Shrubs and Trees of the Southwest Uplands

written by
Francis H. Elmore

drawings by
Jeanne R. Janish

Library of Congress Catalog Card Number: 76-14115

ISBN Number: 0-911408-41-X
Fourth Printing, 1987 - 10,000

Popular Series No. 19

Southwest Parks and Monuments Association
221 North Court, Tucson, Arizona 85701

Printed in the United States of America

9263

Contents

Shrubby Cinquefoil: Cover Photo by Larry Ulrich

1

General Area Map

Shrubs and trees described in this book are found in the general range covered by the shaded portion; however, many may be found in the extended range within the dotted line.

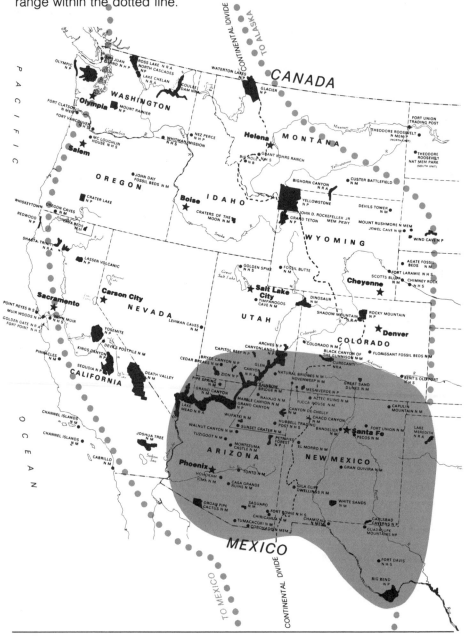

Foreword

Francis H. Elmore is particularly well qualified to author this book. He is a graduate of the University of Southern California with an A. B. degree (Cum Laude) in Botany and a M. S. degree in Archeology and Anthropology. His Master's Thesis, *Ethnobotany of the Navajo* was published as a Monograph of the University of New Mexico and the School of American Research. Francis has had considerable experience in both writing and field work, having worked for the National Park Service for over 30 years, first as a seasonal employee at Bandelier, Chaco Canyon, Casa Grande and Saguaro National Monuments, and as a permanent employee at Chaco Canyon National Monument and Yellowstone and Glacier National Parks as well as at the Natchez Trace Parkway. He was Chief Park Naturalist in Glacier for 12 years.

These varying assignments have given him a thorough acquaintance, not only with the shrubs and trees of our Uplands, but also of the vast contiguous areas.

We are fortunate, too, in having Jeanne R. Janish again to illustrate the *Southwest Uplands,* her fourth illustrated book in the "Southwest" series. Jeanne is exceptionally well qualified, as she has been illustrating for over 50 years, doing over 11,000 scientific drawings in more than 30 books.

All color photographs are by the author except aspen grove, ponderosa pine and redbud by Jeanne R. Janish and Pinyon-Juniper Belt by Betty Jackson.

Earl Jackson, Executive Director
Southwest Parks and Monuments Association

August 1, 1976

Introduction

The Southwest is many things to many people: to some, a hot, dry desert devoid of life or inhabited only by cowboys and Indians or cacti and coyotes; to others, a land of clear skies, picturesque scenery, warm air and abundant sunshine; and to still others, (including us), one of lofty, cool mountains and unexcelled skiing. In other words, the Southwest can be a state of mind, conjured up by the eye of the beholder.

It is the uplands in which we are interested — a vast area with much diversity of soil, climate and altitudinal range — the forested slopes from about 4,500 feet to treeline at about 11,500 feet. Here, low mesas, lofty peaks, deep canyons and shallow arroyos make for some of the most spectacular scenery in the United States.

Shrubs and trees receive much less attention than they deserve, but help make these vistas magnificent: in summer and spring, a glorious green; and in winter, a wonderland of white set off by stately green trees. Surprisingly enough, Arizona is almost 26% forested, New Mexico nearly 27%, Colorado about 30%, Utah about 30%, and even Texas is 22% forested — literally millions of acres of natural scenic beauty. This, then is the Southwest to which you will be introduced.

For our purposes, THE SOUTHWEST UPLANDS (really a region without boundaries) is a vast, sprawling land, stretching from the Mexican boundary and southwest Texas, to well over 500 miles northward to southern Utah and southern Colorado, including all or parts of five states: Arizona, New Mexico, southern Colorado, southern Utah and a portion of western Texas between Old and New Mexico. And because of the limitations placed by the very title, the 4,500-foot contour has arbitrarily been selected as defining the beginning of the Uplands. This, then, further limits the Southwest in which we are interested to the higher areas of these states above the deserts.

The Southwest Uplands, could, for our purposes, also be defined to include all areas drained by the upper portion of the Rio Grande and its tributary, the Pecos; and by the Colorado River south of Grand Junction, Colorado, and its main tributaries, the Gunnison, San Juan and Little Colorado.

Most of us, when we travel, often wonder about the shrubs and trees we see along the roadsides. This book will help you find out more about these Southwest "residents." It sums up what many before have studied and observed. Its aim is to satisfy some of your curiosity while you roam the Southwest. Our modern, paved highway systems have made it easier for you to travel the country and see many areas heretofore nearly inaccessible.

As you travel the Uplands, you cannot help but notice changes in plant life as you ascend — going up 1000 feet in elevation is equivalent to traveling north about 600 miles. In other words, if you were to leave Santa Fe, New Mexico (elev. 7,000 feet) and climb to the top of Santa Fe Baldy (12,622 feet), it would be the same as if you had traveled north to the Arctic Circle, about 3,400 miles. You would also get 3 degrees cooler for each of the thousand feet you climbed — 17 degrees cooler at the top of Baldy than in Santa Fe. This would also mean that in May, when spring arrives in the lowlands, the snows at higher elevations would be just melting, with spring arriving not until late August in the highest Uplands.

This increase in elevation, as well as in coolness, and consequent wetness, divides the Uplands into "belts," each of which contains certain characteristic plants. As each belt has a different set of conditions that predetermines the kinds of plants (and animals) which can live in its region (soil: type, drainage, alkalinity, etc.; climate: temperature, humidity, moisture, wind; others: exposure, light, elevation), both plants and animals adapt themselves to conform to these various conditions, which, in total, are called "environment." Each belt has its own special requirements for growth, and in each habitat live only those plants and animals that can endure its harshest conditions, for example: sagebrush grows a long tap root to reach underground water; manzanita has waxy leaves to prevent moisture loss; quaking aspen and other broadleaved trees shed their leaves after their growth periods; and pinyon and juniper grow in open ranks because of limited water supply.

On your trek upward (if you started from the desert), you would ascend through four vegetative types: pinyon-juniper, pine-oak, fir-aspen and spruce-fir to treeline. In the Southwest Uplands the boundaries of these bands of vegetation are relatively indistinct, and the elevations of each belt increase slightly from north to south. Also the zonal vegetation extends higher on the relatively warmer and drier south and southwest exposures, while the vegetation drops lower on the cooler and moister north and northeast slopes, as well as in cool, shaded canyons. The lower limits of the ponderosa pine and Gambel oak, for instance, may be interspersed with pinyon and juniper, and the upper limits by Douglas-fir and aspen.

For the Southwest Uplands, the first vegetative type we are interested in is the pinyon-juniper belt (Upper Sonoran Zone), roughly from 4,500 feet to 6,500 feet in elevation (p. 13). It is very dry (but not so dry as the desert below), with scattered stands of pinyon and juniper interspersed with sagebrush, rabbitbrush and other drought-resisting species.

Above this belt occurs the ponderosa pine-Gambel oak belt (Transition Life Zone), roughly from about 6,500 feet to 8,000 feet in elevation (p. 109). It is a relatively warm and dry belt, with open stands of ponderosa pine and Apache pine (in Arizona), and in places interspersed with Rocky Mountain juniper. The most characteristic shrubs of this belt are antelopebrush, mountain-mahogany and serviceberry.

Progressing upward, we next find the Douglas-fir-aspen belt (sometimes called the Montane Forest or Canadian Life Zone), from approximately 8,000 feet to 9,500 feet in elevation (p. 157). Here Douglas-fir and quaking aspen reach their height of development and are called "forest indicators." White fir and common juniper also occur in this forest type. Only the most tolerant shrubs can endure in the subdued light under the heavy tree cover, among them, the honeysuckles are the most conspicuous.

Between about 9,500 feet and 11,500 feet, the spruce-fir belt appears (p. 173). This has also been called Subalpine Forest and Hudsonian Life Zone. Here forests of Engelmann spruce, subalpine fir and corkbark fir (in Arizona) occur, and extend to treeline. Toward the upper reaches of the forest, vegetation becomes stunted and dwarfed, the trees assuming distorted growth due to the nearly constant strong winds so frequent at these high altitudes. Blueberry and waxflower are the characteristic shrubs of this belt. Limber and bristlecone pines are also found here, with the bristlecone having a scattered distribution on widely separated high peaks throughout the Uplands.

At around 11,500 feet, treeline itself is reached, with its gnarled and twisted trees (p. 186). This is the frontier at which fullsize trees cannot grow, and marks the beginning of the alpine tundra.

Scheme of Things

This little book is intended not only to supplement, but also to extend the coverage of the triad of earlier books: Dodge and Janish *Flowers of the Southwest Deserts* covering plants below 4,500 feet in elevation; Patraw and Janish *Flowers of the Southwest Mesas* treating the pinyon-juniper belt; and Arnberger and Janish *Flowers of the Southwest Mountains* embracing our other three belts. All, of necessity, included some shrubs and trees.

The present book was specifically written as a guide to the identification of the shrubs and trees of the Southwest Uplands, and consequently incorporates some of the shrubs and trees from all three books. These have been redescribed (and some redrawn) afresh in order that all of the more common shrubs and trees from 4,500 feet upward be included. They are, in general, the most representative of all the genera (plural of genus) within the Uplands. The list therefore, is not exhaustive, nor is it intended to be. One hundred and sixty-eight species and varieties are described. Only the conifers have been fully treated (23 species and varieties).

The writing has been made as nontechnical as possible to provide a ready means of identification for the more common shrubs and trees. Of course, not all of the species described are to be found in all five states, but the great majority of them occur in at least three.

Two common species, tamarisk and Russian-olive, so often seen in the Southwest have been included although they are not native to the United States, having been introduced years ago. They have become "naturalized" over the years, thus appear to be "natives" to many.

It is hoped that this little book will assist you in identifying an unknown shrub or tree. This may be done easiest by flipping through the color-coded pages, especially those for the belt which you assume you are in. In order to further simplify things, no technical keys are provided; however, for the conifers, an identification chart and a simple key are provided.

The descriptive text is divided into several parts: first, the more accepted common name at the top of the page in heavy type, and beneath, in smaller type, any local names or any of Spanish-American origin; next, under the illustration is the scientific (Latin) name and the family to which it belongs. There is still some disagreement among botanists about Latin names. For trees the U. S. Forest Service *Check List* has been used as our authority; and for shrubs, Kearney and Peebles *Arizona Flora* is used where applicable; otherwise we hope that the proper Latin name has been used, sometimes over three or four synonyms used by various authors, and that the "soundest" has been chosen. "Latin" name in some cases is a Greek, Arabic or French name, but all latinized, of course. Even Carib and Japanese names creep in.

Species names are even more mixed up; some authors "splitting" and others "lumping." Oaks are the best example. Based on leaf characteristics, several "species" of oaks were described; however, it was found that, based on the leaf characteristics alone, *two or more species* could be found growing on the same tree!

"Range" is a separate paragraph broken into several parts: our range, range extension, type of habitat and minimum and maximum elevational limits. "Our whole range" means that the shrub or tree occurs in Arizona, New Mexico, southern Utah, southern Colorado and western Texas, but not necessarily covering the whole area, as the belts are not contiguous and the plants have a very scattered distribution. Beyond our range this book should still be useful, especially in the adjacent states of California, Nevada, Idaho, Wyoming, Nebraska, Kansas and Oklahoma and north to Montana and Canada as well as contiguous Old Mexico. These extended ranges are indicated as "s. to Mex.," "n. to Can.," etc., indicating that the species also ranges southward *into* Mexico, northward *into* Canada, etc. The two-letter contractions for the states conform to the official United States Postal Service abbreviations. For other countries, commonly accepted abbreviations as Can., Mex., Alta., Nfld. and Eu. for Canada, Mexico, Alberta, Newfoundland and Europe are used. A list of these, and other abbreviations used appears on p. 203. Elevation figures given under *"Range"* are for the Southwest Uplands — Douglas-fir, for example, grows at sea level in Oregon, and aspen at sea level in Alaska, but in our more southerly climates grow above 4,000 feet and 6,000 feet respectively.

Shrub or Tree?

The time-honored definition of a tree is: a woody plant having one well-defined trunk at least two inches in diameter, a height of at least ten feet, and a somewhat definitely formed crown of foliage. Conversely, a shrub would have more than one stem, each less than two inches in diameter, a height of less than ten feet, and an undefined crown. A more broad definition would be: if you can walk *under* it, it is a tree, but if you have to walk *around* it, it is a shrub.

As with all generalizations, there are exceptions; notably, the Engelmann spruce, which, at treeline becomes a prostrate, matted shrub, (p. 108) and coyote and Scouler willows which usually are shrubs with clustered stems, but may become treelike.

Included in this book are four "woody" vines: Alpine clematis, canyon grape, Virginia creeper, and western virgin's bower, which technically are neither shrubs nor trees. A few plants classed as "subshrubby," "shrublike," or "partly woody" have also been included.

Wildlife Sanctuaries

In the Southwest Uplands are to be found some of the most scenic lands in America. Through the National Park Service many of these areas are being preserved for you and yours in perpetuity.

The idea of setting aside land areas of superb scenery (including wildlife — plants as well as animals) for permanent preservation in their primeval condition was first expressed in the law that established Yellowstone National Park in 1872. In 1906 provision was made for the creation of National Monuments, but it was not until 1916 that the National Park Service, as such, was established. Today, nearly 300 units of various types are included in the Park system. Of these, about 40 are within our Uplands. Each is of outstanding national significance.

Through these basic laws, sanctuaries were provided for all wildlife, thus safeguarding it for all time for the benefit and enjoyment not only for the present-day visitors, but for the generations to come. Vegetation is one of the primary scenic and scientific features for which these areas were established. It is a priceless resource, for birds and animals depend on it for support and survival.

Here you can enjoy a relatively unspoiled landscape dominated by shrubs and trees. Photograph freely, but remember, picking wildflowers and other plants cannot be allowed. Because thousands before you were thoughtful enough not to have picked or damaged the plants and other natural features, they are here now so that you, too, may enjoy them. Please leave them undisturbed for the thousands who will follow you.

Acknowledgments

Both the author and the illustrator gratefully acknowledge, with sincere appreciation, the invaluable help of the following persons:

Dr. Charles T. Mason, Jr., Curator of the Herbarium, College of Agriculture, The University of Arizona, Tucson, for his painstaking review of the manuscript, for his many excellent suggestions and for loaning herbarium sheets from the University herbarium.

Dr. William A. Weber, Curator of Botany, University of Colorado, Boulder, who not only was extremely helpful, but allowed free access to the over-280,000 specimens in the University herbarium and loaned numerous herbarium specimens.

Dr. Wesley Niles, Associate Professor of Biology, The University of Nevada at Las Vegas was most helpful and cooperative in loaning books as well as herbarium specimens.

Dr. D. J. Pinkava, Associate Professor and Mrs. Elinor Lehto, Herbarium Curator, both of the Department of Botany and Microbiology, Arizona State University, Tempe for loan of several herbarium specimens and for use of their personal libraries.

Dr. John Hunter Thomas of Stanford University, California and Dr. William G. Gambill, Jr., Director of the Denver Botanic Gardens for personal loans of not-readily-available publications.

Dr. Charlotte Donskey, Chairperson, Department of Modern Languages and Literature, Regis College, Denver, Colorado who not only helped greatly with the Latin, but also condoned my fractured Latin as suitable for the layman; however, for any offbeat pronunciations or obvious mistakes, I take full responsibility.

The author is deeply indebted to the gifted Jeanne R. Janish for consenting to come out of "retirement" to do the illustrations for this book. She was untiring in her efforts to assure that the drawings were scientifically accurate, and very helpful in her many suggestions for the "thumbnail" sketches included on the plates. They not only add greatly to the clarification of the drawings, but also eased my burden of providing textual material. It was a gratifying and pleasurable experience to be able to work with such an outstanding artist as Jeanne.

Ten illustrations (golden rabbitbrush, longflower snowberry, big and bud sagebrush, Utah juniper, singleleaf pinyon, curlleaf mountain-mahogany, fernbush, limber pine and bristlecone pine) are from *Death Valley Wildflowers* (Copyright 1974) by Roxana S. Ferris with illustrations by Jeanne R. Janish, and are used with permission of the Death Valley Natural History Association, G. Frank Ackerman, Executive Secretary.

The drawing of *Arctostaphylos uva-ursi* is from *Flowers of the Point Reyes National Seashore* (1970) by Roxana S. Ferris and illustrated by Jeanne R. Janish. It was originally published by the University of California Press; reprinted by permission of The Regents of the University of California.

To my wife I express sincere thanks for her constant help throughout in checking the manuscript and proofs and for her many excellent suggestions, arduous tasks that greatly improved the final product.

And last, but not least, Earl Jackson, Executive Director, Southwest Parks and Monuments Association who not only encouraged and advised, but also offered many helpful suggestions and saw this book through the press to full fruition.

August 1, 1976

Francis H. Elmore

Francis H. Elmore
Northglenn, Colorado

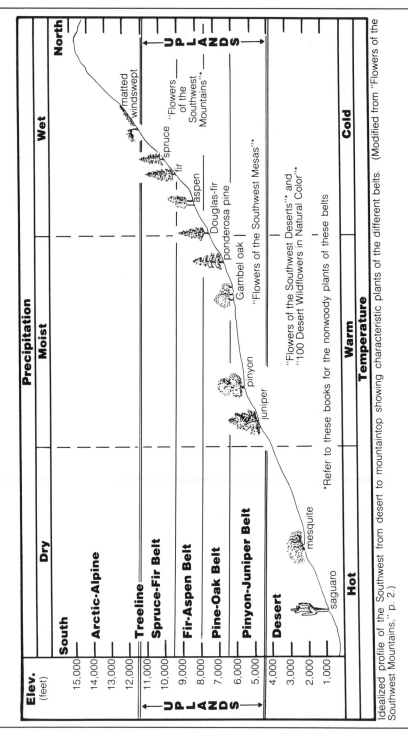

Elev. (feet)	Dry	Precipitation Moist	Wet

South — North

	Temperature	
Hot	Warm	Cold

Arctic-Alpine

15,000
14,000
13,000
12,000 — **Treeline**
11,000 — **Spruce-Fir Belt**
10,000
9,000 — **Fir-Aspen Belt**
8,000
7,000 — **Pine-Oak Belt**
6,000
5,000 — **Pinyon-Juniper Belt**
4,000
3,000 — **Desert**
2,000
1,000

←U P L A N D S→

matted
windswept

spruce

fir

aspen

Douglas-fir
ponderosa pine

Gambel oak

pinyon

juniper

mesquite

saguaro

"Flowers
of the
Southwest
Mountains"*

"Flowers of the Southwest Mesas"*

"Flowers of the Southwest Deserts"* and
"100 Desert Wildflowers in Natural Color"*

*Refer to these books for the nonwoody plants of these belts

Idealized profile of the Southwest from desert to mountaintop showing characteristic plants of the different belts. (Modified from "Flowers of the Southwest Mountains," p. 2.)

Pinyon-Juniper Belt

(Approx. 4,500' - 6,500' elev.)

Here, between the deserts below and the forests above, pinyon pines and junipers grow closely associated and dominate the landscape (p. 94). This land of the pinyon and juniper which covers some 40,000 square miles, lies scattered throughout most of Arizona and New Mexico north of the desert regions; it includes large areas in western and southwestern Colorado, especially along the courses of the Colorado and Gunnison Rivers and their tributaries; it embraces portions of southern Utah between the Colorado and San Juan Rivers, and west to the Virgin River drainage; it takes in parts of the bordering states of Nevada, Oklahoma and Texas, and sections of Old Mexico as well.

The widely spaced, open, mixed stands of pinyon and juniper give this belt a distinctive individuality entirely different from that of any other. In places, pinyon and juniper are equal in numbers; at others, one species is dominant over the other. Usually at lower elevations juniper is more abundant, and at the higher upper limits it thins out and pinyon becomes the more common tree, sometimes occurring in almost solid stands of considerable extent. These relatively small trees are not so tall as those of the higher mountains. Because of this, the name "Dwarf or Pygmy Forest" is sometimes applied to these wooded areas which cover millions of acres in the Southwest.

This belt has been variously called Upper Sonoran Zone, Plains Zone or Woodlands Zone. It ranges from the high plains and foothills in the south to the low plains and foothill canyons in the north. For our purposes, the elevations between 4,500 and 6,500 feet have been chosen as the lower and upper boundaries of the belt. As occurs in all belts, there is some overlapping of species from the lower and upper belts.

The terrain is usually dry and rocky or gravelly, and characterized by limited moisture. The average annual precipitation is between 10 and 20 inches. Summer days are often hot (but not so hot as in the drier desert immediately below). Winters are relatively long and see some snowfall. Rainfall throughout this belt is scanty, thereby restricting the plants mostly to drought-resisting species.

Besides the pinyon pine and the Utah juniper, singleleaf and Mexican pinyons and alligator and one-seed junipers are found in this belt. Desert species such as shadscale, saltbush and greasewood are intermixed with the junipers and pinyons, especially where the soil tends toward alkalinity.

Cacti and yuccas creep upward into the lower reaches, and scraggly ponderosa pines edge downward into the upper border along with Gambel oaks. In the southern part of our area the Chihuahua pine can be found.

Sagebrush is frequently interspersed with pinyon and juniper, often taking over acre upon acre of land unbroken by even a single tree. Along the streams grow cottonwoods, walnuts and sycamores, while on drier sites you can find shrubs such as rabbitbrush, fernbush, cliffrose, Apache-plume, squawbush and scrub oak, any of which may assume local dominance.

A total of 89 species is listed in this section, of which over 78% can be found in the deserts below. Creeping down into this belt from the three higher belts are about 50 species of shrubs and trees, besides 9 conifers.

Pinyon

pinyon pine, nut pine, piñón

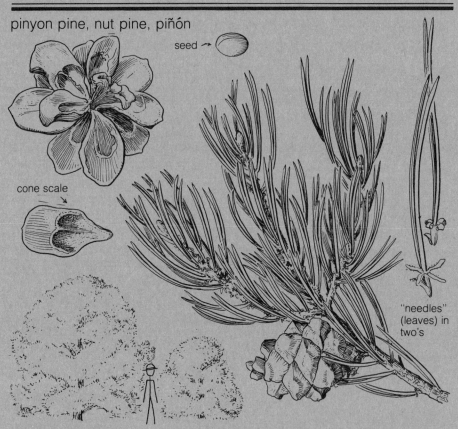

seed

cone scale

"needles" (leaves) in two's

Pinus edulis

Pine family *(Pinaceae)*

Range: Our whole range; n. to WY; s. to Mex. Dry, rocky places, 4,000' - 8,000'.

Pinyon, New Mexico's picturesque state tree, often has a crooked trunk with reddish bark, and grows, at most, 35 feet tall. It occurs in either pure stands or intermixed with Utah juniper. Growth is very slow, and trees 6 to 10 inches in diameter may be 100 to 150 years old.

The chunky little cones (p. 105) produce the well-known tasty pinyon nuts. They are some of the largest nuts produced by any of our pines and are sold throughout the country as pinyon or pine nuts, Indian nuts, or Christmas nuts. Periodically bumper crops of these delicious seeds are produced and avidly gathered by the natives — if the small animals and birds don't get there first! Occasionally woodrats' nests are robbed for their stored nuts, sometimes yielding up to 30 pounds.

The tree is highly prized for providing pitchy, fragrant firewood.

Utah Juniper

western juniper, sabina, "cedro"

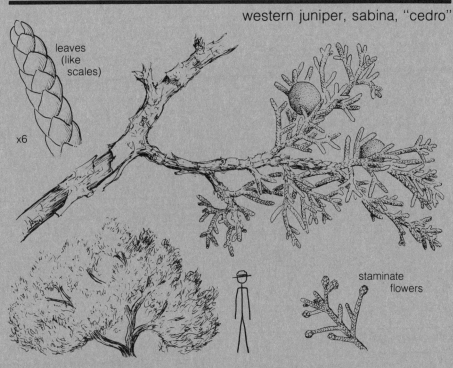

leaves
(like
scales)

x6

staminate
flowers

Juniperus osteosperma   Cypress family *(Cupressaceae)*

Range: AZ, NM, CO, UT; w. to CA; n. to ID & WY. Dry, rocky places, 3,000' - 8,000'.

   This juniper is usually quite bushy and freely branched, growing no higher than about 15 feet nor more than 12 inches in diameter. Together with the pinyon (opposite), it is the most predominant species of tree in the Southwest, covering millions of acres, growing intermixed with it throughout the pinyon-juniper belt.

   Its appearance is similar to that of the one-seed juniper, and the two are hard to tell apart. If the "berries" are handy to compare, those of the Utah juniper are marble size, reddish brown or bluish with a powdery coating (p. 96) and mealy and fibrous; those of the one-seed juniper are pea size, copper colored or blue and succulent when fresh. The one-seed juniper almost always has several branches arising from the ground, whereas the Utah juniper has a definite trunk.

   The Hopi Indians use the Utah juniper for medicine and ceremonial purposes and the berries for beads. The Navajo Indians use the wood for hogans, firewood and fenceposts, and the shreddy bark for bedding.

Alligator Juniper

alligator- or checkered-bark juniper; western juniper; cedro chino [rough (-barked) "cedar"]

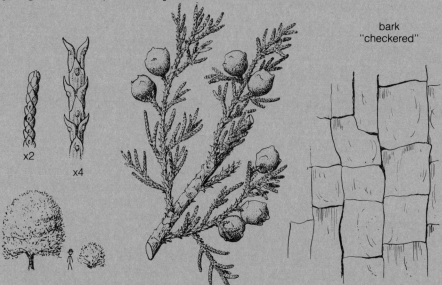

bark "checkered"

Juniperus deppeana   Cypress family *(Cupressaceae)*

Range: AZ, NM, w. TX; s. to Mex. Dry hills & mesas, 4,500' - 8,000'.

There is no doubting the alligator juniper when it is first seen. Its thick, deeply furrowed, red brown bark is broken into small squared plates 1 to 2 inches across, like an alligator's skin. It usually grows to tree size, about 20 to 40 feet tall, but sometimes is only a large spreading shrub. Its trunk may reach a diameter of 2 to 3 feet — the latter size being from 500 to 800 years old.

If the tree is not mature enough to have checkered bark, then you're in trouble. Look closely at the needles and berries; its scalelike leaves are more pointed and less closely pressed to the stem than in other tree junipers; its foliage more dense and thickly dotted with resin. Its marble-size berries usually have 4 seeds (other junipers have from 1 to 3), are bluish gray and fleshy, but turn red brown on maturing.

As with other junipers, its berries are an important source of food for birds and animals. Many Indian tribes ate them too, either fresh or dried and stored them for winter use.

The wood is used locally for fuel and fenceposts, although that of other species seems to be preferred, probably because they are more common.

When first discovered by American expeditions to the Southwest in the 1850s, it was described as a very peculiar tree, having bark like that of an oak, but limbs of a juniper.

One-seed Juniper

cherry-stone or redberry juniper; sabina

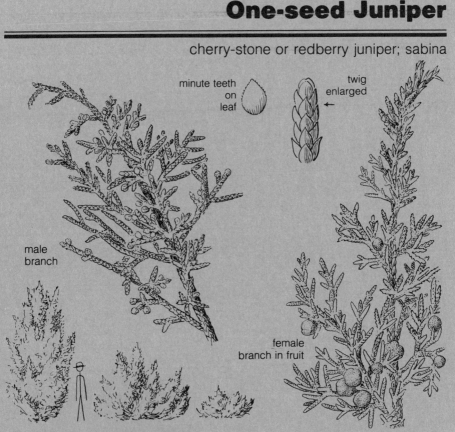

minute teeth on leaf

twig enlarged

male branch

female branch in fruit

Juniperus monosperma   Cypress family *(Cupressaceae)*

Range: Our whole range; w. to NV; n. to WY; e. to OK; s. to Mex. Dry hills & mesas, 3,500' - 8,000'.

   The characteristic juniper of northern Arizona and New Mexico, intermixes with pinyon pine. It is more shrubby than other junipers, having several stems, and growing to a maximum height of about 20 feet and about a foot in diameter. (See Utah juniper, p. 15).
   The berries are copper color (rarely bluish), succulent and unappetizing, but can be eaten if need be (the Indians ate them!). The berry is usually one seeded, but occasionally two seeded. The Spanish name for the berry is nebrina.
   The Navajo made use of its bark (garments, blankets, sandals), wood (firewood, fenceposts, hogans), twigs (prayersticks, stirrers), seeds (necklaces, anklets, wristlets), medicine (cure for "flu"), gum (chewing gum) and bark and berries (green dye). Its shreddy bark makes an excellent kindling for starting campfires.

Singleleaf Pinyon

one-leaf or single-leaf pinyon pine (piñón), nut pine

1 in.

leaves,
natural
size

Pinus monophylla

Pine family *(Pinaceae)*

Range: nw AZ, w. UT; w. to CA; n. to ID; s. to Mex. Coarse, gravelly soils, 2,000' - 8,000'.

On the 24th day of January in the year of 1844, Captain John C. Frémont in his *Report of the Exploring Expedition to Oregon and North California in the years 1843-'44,* first described the singleleaf pinyon: " . . .today we saw for the first time, and which Dr. [John] Torrey has described as a new species, under the name of *pinus monophyllus* [sic]; in popular language . . .the *nut pine.*"

Unique among all the pines is this species — its needles occurring singly, not in bundles of 2 to 5 as in all other pines. Some authorities list the singleleaf pinyon (1 needle), the pinyon pine (2 needles), and the Parry pine (4 needles) as varieties of the Mexican pinyon (3 needles). Its distribution is quite different from that of the Mexican pinyon, overlapping it not at all.

Singleleaf pinyon has some use for corrals, fenceposts and fuel, but its main use is for food — the nuts are eaten either raw or roasted. Frémont described the nut as " . . .oily, of very agreeable flavor, and must be very nutritious, as it constitutes the principal subsistence of the tribes among which we were now travelling." [The Expedition was then in the vicinity of present-day Carson City, Nevada, named for "Kit" Carson, Frémont's guide].

Mexican Pinyon

three-leaved or stoneseed pinyon pine; piñón

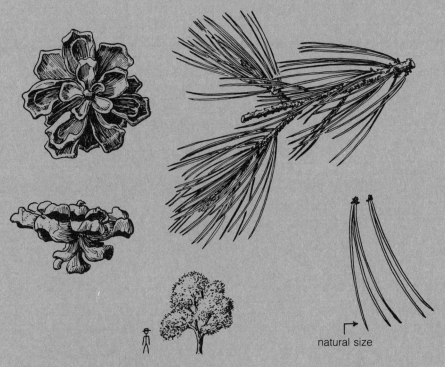

natural size

Pinus cembroides

Pine family *(Pinaceae)*

Range: se AZ, sw NM, w. TX; s. to Mex. Dry hills & mesas, 4,800' - 8,000'.

This pinyon is easily recognized because it is the only one with 3 needles from 1 to 2 inches long. The yellow-blotched, chocolate brown cones are quite irregular and stubby, have relatively few cone scales and are no more than 2 inches high. Its seeds are extensively gathered and sold in the native markets throughout Mexico where they are highly esteemed for their unexcelled sweet oily nutty flavor. They are good raw, but the flavor is greatly improved by roasting. They are the largest of the pinyon nuts, reaching ½ to ¾ inch in size.

The Mexicans become very adept (and "norteamericanos" too, with practice) at placing a handful of pinyon nuts in the mouth, cracking them with the teeth, and ejecting the hulls out one side of the mouth while stashing the nuts in the opposite cheek.

A tree 20 feet high is unusual, and may be from 250 to 350 years old.

Some authorities recognize only this species of pinyon, the 1- and 2-needle pinyons being classed as varieties of this one.

Chihuahua Pine

ocote blancc [white pitch pine], ocote chino [rough (-barked) pitch pine], pino real; "yellow pine"

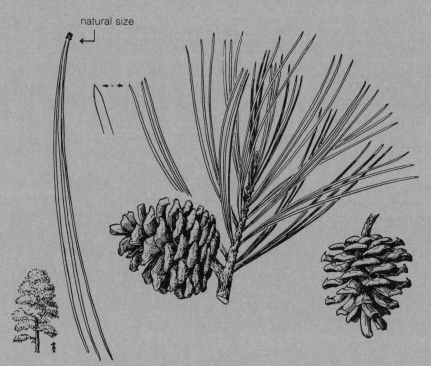

natural size

Pinus leiophylla **var. chihuahuana** Pine family *(Pinaceae)*

Range: se AZ, sw NM; s. to Mex. Dry slopes & benches, 5,000' - 8,200'.

A relatively small pine tree, 35 to 50 feet tall and about 2 feet in diameter and of limited distribution in the United States. Its needles occur in bundles of 3 and are slender, pale waxy green, and from 2 to 4 inches long. The sheaths at the bases of the needle bundles, unlike other pines, are shed.

The cones are about 1½ to 2½ inches long, light chestnut brown in color and dull glossy. The cones remain on the trees for years.

Young twigs are orange brown, but, with age, turn dull red brown. The bark consists of scales which are brownish black, broken by red brown grooves.

The yellowish male flowers and the greenish female flowers do not appear until July, producing a fall crop of pine nuts. The nuts are tiny (about ⅛ inch) as compared to the Mexican pinyon seeds which are from ½ to ¾ inch in size.

The best place to see this pine in the United States is at Chiricahua National Monument in southern Arizona.

Tamarisk

salt-"cedar," tamarisco, tamariz, pino salado

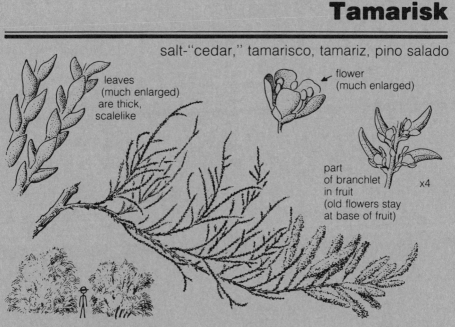

leaves (much enlarged) are thick, scalelike

flower (much enlarged)

part of branchlet in fruit (old flowers stay at base of fruit)

x4

Tamarix pentandra

Tamarisk family *(Tamaricaceae)*

Range: Our whole range; w. to CA; n. to ND; e. to FL; s. to Mex. Sandy, moist soils, especially alkaline soils; riverbanks, streambeds, lakeshores, irrigation ditches, wells and springs, low undrained areas, 3,500' - 6,000'.

In spring and most of summer, tamarisk bears large clusters of showy, pink, tiny flowers in profusion, giving the tree a very wispy-hazy-feathery appearance. Its delicate, wiry, drooping branches are covered with tiny, grayish green scalelike leaves and resemble somewhat the long, slender branchlets of "cedar" (juniper).

It would be classed as a small tree, growing normally to only about 15 to 20 feet high; however, the largest measured tamarisk is in Albuquerque, New Mexico, presumably growing under ideal conditions. It is 44 feet tall with a trunk diameter of over 2 feet.

The tamarisk is a native of Arabian and mideastern deserts, but came to us by way of the Mediterranean countries. Because of its beautiful feathery flowers, it was introduced as a shade tree and for hedges. It was also planted for erosion control; however, where it has escaped it sometimes becomes a pest not only because it is hard to eradicate once it has established itself, but also because it uses so much water so vitally needed by other native plants.

Birds and small animals have readily adapted themselves to this intruder, using it for nesting sites and for protective cover. The Ord kangaroo rat has been recorded as eating tamarisk seeds and foliage. Even honeybees have learned that its tiny flowers are a good source of nectar.

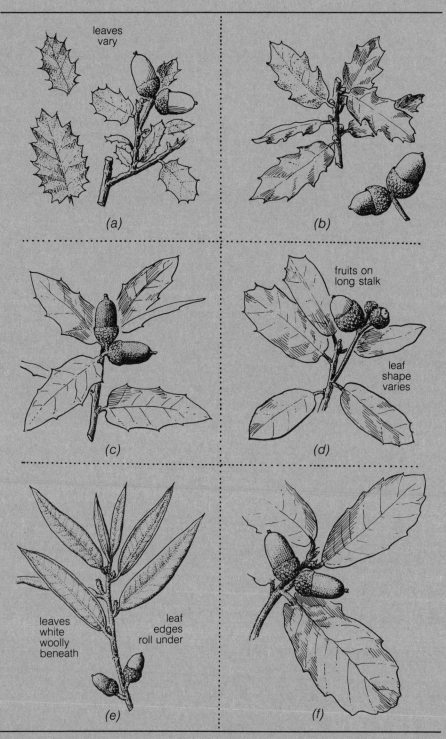

leaves
vary

(a)

(b)

(c)

fruits on
long stalk

leaf
shape
varies

(d)

leaves
white
woolly
beneath

leaf
edges
roll under

(e)

(f)

Oaks

robles, encinas, encinos, belloteros [acorn-trees]

Quercus species

Beech family *(Fagaceae)*

The oak has long been considered a symbol of strength ("sturdy as an oak," "mighty oaks from little acorns grow"), and is celebrated in myths and legends throughout the world. It was sacred to Thor and Jupiter, while the Druids, who thought that it inspired prophecy, built their altars under it.

Indians and Spanish-Americans alike gathered acorns for food.

Many birds and animals eat its acorns, and mule deer and porcupines have been known to eat oak leaves.

Oak wood is used for flooring, furniture, fuel and fenceposts.

Shrub Live Oak *(a)*

scrub oak, encino achaparrado [shrub-size oak]   *Quercus turbinella*
Range: Our whole range; w. to CA; s. to Mex. Dry slopes, 4,500' - 8,000'.
This oak should be readily identified by its small, somewhat shiny, bluish green, hollylike leaves with spine-tipped teeth and dull yellow to reddish, hairy undersides.

Wavyleaf Oak *(b)*

scrub, shin, switch or evergreen oak; encino   *Quercus undulata*
Range: Our whole range; w. to CA; s. to Mex. Dry places, 4,000' - 10,000'.
Wavy leaf margins of this oak are distinctive. The leaves are shiny and blue green and slightly (if at all) crinkled.

Emory Oak *(c)*

black or blackjack oak; roble negro [black oak], bellota   *Quercus emoryi*
Range: c. & se AZ, sw NM, w. TX; s. to Mex. Dry, rocky places, 3,000' - 8,000'.
Stiff, leathery, lustrous, dark green leaves serve to identify this oak. The undersides of the leaves are somewhat paler.

Gray Oak *(d)*   shin oak, encina blanca [white oak]   *Quercus grisea*

Range: s. AZ, s. NM, w. TX; s. to Mex. Dry rocky sites, 4,500' - 7,800'.
Small, oval, usually smooth-margined (occasionally toothed), dusty, gray blue leaves distinguish this oak from all others in our range.

Silverleaf Oak *(e)*

white leaf oak, encino blanco   *Quercus hypoleucoides*
Range: se AZ, sw NM, w. TX; s. to Mex. Slopes & ridges, 4,000' - 8,500'.
This is the only one of our oaks to have silver-felt undersides on its lustrous, dark green leaves and the inside of the acorn cup fuzzy. The small chestnut brown acorn is enclosed for about ⅓ of its length by a silver-haired, scaly cup.

Arizona White Oak *(f)*   Arizona oak, roble   *Quercus arizonica*

Range: c. & se AZ, s. NM, w. TX; s. to Mex. Dry, rocky slopes, 5,000' - 10,000'.
The undersides of this oak's leaves are permanently and densely matted with short, fuzzy, light brown hairs. Their upper surfaces are dull bluish green. The *insides* of the acorn cups are also fuzzy. The "evergreen" leaves are dropped before the new leaves emerge.

Western Virgin's Bower

traveler's-joy, old-man's-beard, barba de chivo [goat's beard], yerba de chivato [he-goat herb], clemátide, muermera

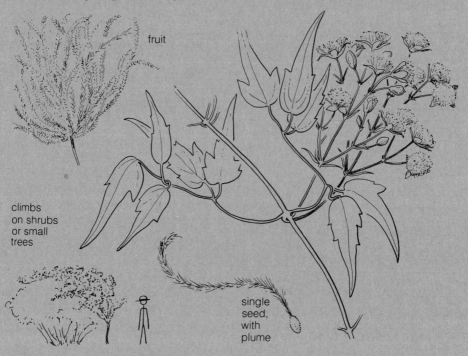

fruit

climbs
on shrubs
or small
trees

single
seed,
with
plume

Clematis ligusticifolia   Buttercup family *(Ranunculaceae)*

Range: Our whole range; w. to CA; n. to Can. Brushy hillsides and streamsides, 3,000' - 8,500'.

One of four "woody" vines in our range — the others are Alpine clematis in the fir-aspen belt, Virginia creeper in the pine-oak belt, and canyon grape (opposite).

Instantly recognizable in the fall because of the conspicuous fluffy white balls covering the female vine (p. 97). It sprawls over bushes, trees, rocks or anything handy, so that it looks as if the supporting object were in full fruit rather than the clematis. The flowers have no petals, but the 4 sepals are petal-like, creamy white and rather showy, but are only about 1 inch across. Tendril-like leaf stems with 5 leaflets help it climb, sometimes from 20 to 40 feet.

Male and female flowers grow on separate plants.

Indians and settlers alike chewed the plant as a sore throat and cold remedy. Cuts and sores on horses were treated with an infusion of the leaves. Clematis-seed poultices were used on burns.

Canyon Grape

Arizona grape, vid [Sp: vine, esp. the grape vine], parra cimarrona [wild grape vine]

petal
cap

Vitis arizonica

Grape family *(Vitaceae)*

Range: Our whole range (CO?); w. to CA; s. to Mex. Near watercourses in canyons, gulches and ravines, 2,000' - 7,500'.

There is no mistaking this wild grape with its large (1½ to 3¼ inches) maplelike leaves, shreddy bark, coiling branched tendrils, and, in season, clusters of juicy black purple fruits. It climbs over bushes, small trees and rocks.

Throughout the centuries, in literature and in art, the grape has been a symbol of revelry and joy, and contributed to many a bacchanalian bash. Our canyon grape is no exception. The fruits mature in July and August, and even though they have a very tart flavor and are not very palatable when eaten from the vine, they make fine jellies, preserves, grape juice and wine. Grape pie is made occasionally from the fresh or dried grapes. Even the tendrils can be eaten raw for a distinctively different tidbit.

Canyon grape flowers are very small and white and appear in clusters opposite the leaves. It is interesting to note that a "petal-cap" comes off in one piece, exposing the stamens.

The Pueblo Indians cultivated the vine for its fruits which they ate raw or sun dried them for later use.

Wild grapes are eaten by many small animals, as well as by almost 100 species of birds, some using the bark for nests.

Poison Ivy

poison-sumac(h), hiedra (yedra) mala [evil vine]

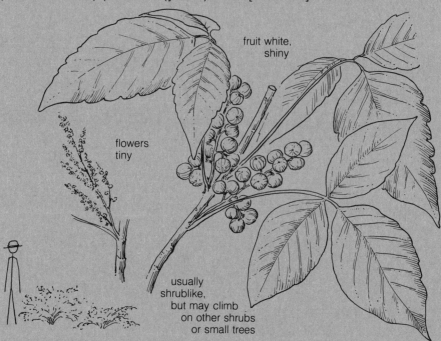

fruit white, shiny

flowers tiny

usually shrublike, but may climb on other shrubs or small trees

Rhus radicans   Cashew or Sumac family *(Anacardiaceae)*

Range: Our whole range; throughout most of the U.S.; n. to Can.; s. to Mex. & W. Indies. Shady woods, esp. in disturbed soils, 3,000' - 8,000'.

You may have wondered why your favorite picnic spot was becoming overrun by poison ivy. It seems to have an affinity for disturbed areas, and picnic areas are quickly trampled down and "disturbed."

Hardly anyone has not suffered the consequences of brushing against the plant. The milky sap, twigs and fruit, or even breathing the toxin-laden smoke can cause severe, itchy, skin rash — even internal poisoning. Some people are more susceptible than others.

Three, lusterless, oaklike leaves and clusters of globe-shaped, ivory-colored, almost glossy berries help to identify this plant. It is sometimes confused with 5-leaved Virginia creeper (p. 131).

It can either be a low shrub (to 2 feet) or a vine, climbing by aerial rootlets with disklike suckers.

The best advice: AVOID IT, susceptible or not! If, by chance, contact is made, immediately wash the affected parts in water — with strong soap, if possible. For more severe cases, see a doctor.

Squawbush

squaw- or lemonadeberry; aromatic, fragrant, ill-scented, skunkbush, or threeleaf sumac(h); lemita

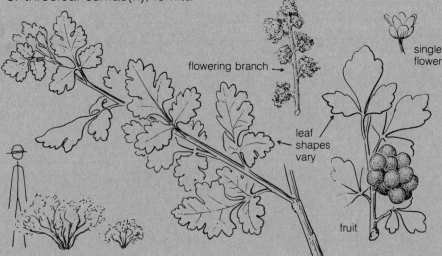

flowering branch →

single flower

leaf shapes vary

fruit

Rhus trilobata   Cashew or Sumac family *(Anacardiaceae)*

Range: Our whole range; w. to CA; n. to Can.; e. to IA; s. to Mex. Dry hillsides, canyons, valleys & plains, 3,500' - 9,000'.

Squawbush is a shrub from about 2 to 6 feet tall with three leaflets, each of which is three lobed, resembling currant leaves.

In spring, tiny clusters of yellowish flowers appear even before the leaves, and by summer, develop into bunches of dark red, sticky, slightly hairy berries. It is these berries that give the name "lemonadeberry" or "limonada" to the bush, as they are used with sugar to make a refreshing lemonadelike drink. They may be rolled around in the mouth as they come off the bush; however, they are quite tart, but a treat on any hot summer day as they allay thirst by stimulating the flow of saliva. They were dried by the Indians for future use and also used as one of the ingredients of pemmican.

When fall arrives, the leaves of squawbush, and the closely related poison ivy (opposite), turn a rich red just before they drop off, adding another brilliant color to the already variegated autumnal hues of the mountainsides.

It is called "squawbush" because Indian women used its stems more extensively than any other plant, except willow, in basketmaking. Aromatic, fragrant, ill-scented and skunkbush are all adjectives describing various persons' reactions to the unique scent given off by the crushed leaves.

Cashew and pistachio nuts and mangoes come from trees of this family.

Birds and small animals eat the berries, rabbits the bark and pronghorn, deer, moose and bighorn sheep, the twigs and foliage.

Smooth Sumac

scarlet, red or white sumac

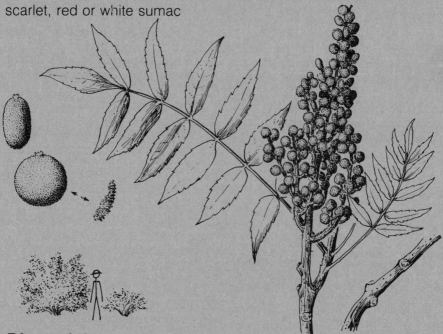

Rhus glabra

Cashew or Sumac family *(Anacardiaceae)*

Range: Our whole range; n. to Can.; e. to Atl. Coast; s. to Mex. Rich, moist, but well-drained soils, 5,000' - 7,500'.

Dark red trusses of glandular fruits easily identify this shrub far into the winter after its leaves have dropped. In the autumn, before the leaves fall, they turn a bright red, scarlet or red violet, adding a brilliant touch of color to the countryside.

The shrub itself grows usually from 3 to 7 feet tall, but may become a small tree up to 20 feet. The dark green leaves are pinnately compound, that is with leaflets on opposite sides of a central leaf stalk (p.95). In this species there are from 4 to 8 pairs of leaflets with a single leaflet at the tip, making a total of 9 to 17 leaflets to each leaf stalk.

The slightly acid berries are used to make "lemonade" when mixed with water and sugar. The pulverized fruits freshen water when added to it.

It forms a good cover for rabbits, chipmunks and other small animals, and provides berries for food. Thirty-two species of birds feed on the fruits. Wild turkeys, quail, bobwhite, pheasants and grouse especially rely on the berries as a winter food.

Smooth sumac was brought under cultivation as early as 1620.

Sumac is a modification of an Arabic word; commonly pronounced SOO-mack, sometimes SHOO-mack. Another spelling is sumach.

Peachleaf Willow

almondleaf, almond or peach willow; sauce

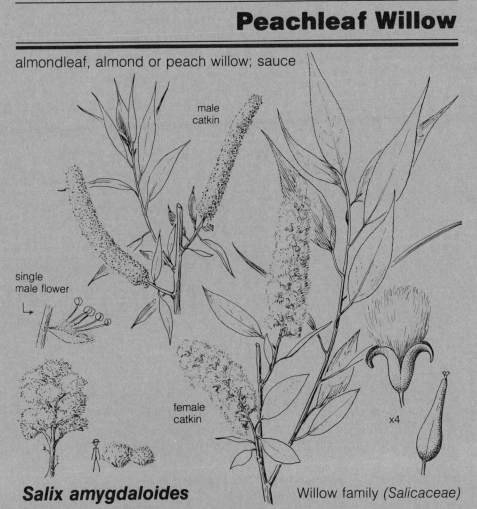

male catkin

single male flower

female catkin

x4

Salix amygdaloides

Willow family *(Salicaceae)*

Range: Our whole range; w. to CA; n. to Can., thence across Can. & n. U.S. to Que. & NY; s. to Mex. Along streambanks, 2,000' - 7,500'.

Peachleaf willow receives its name from the fact that its leaves resemble those of the common peach. It is the most common willow of this belt, and is the only one of the willows covered which can truly merit the name "tree." It normally grows to about 30 feet in height with a trunk diameter of 1 foot; however, it more often occurs in clumps of several spreading individuals.

The bark is normally dark brown, often tinged with red, and irregularly fissured into broad, flat, connected ridges. It often becomes shaggy.

The drooping new twigs are yellow to orange, becoming reddish brown to ash gray upon maturing. The leaves are yellowish green above and paler beneath, with prominent yellow midribs. They are widest at the base and have saw-toothed margins.

Silktassel Bush

yellowleaf silktassel, "quinine-bush"

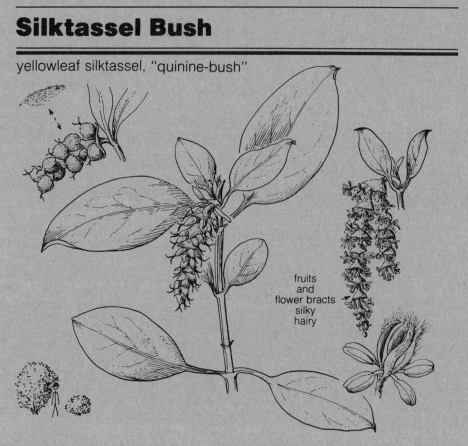

fruits
and
flower bracts
silky
hairy

Garrya flavescens

Dogwood family *(Cornaceae)*

Range: AZ, s. UT, w. TX; w. to CA; s. to Mex. Hillsides & canyons, 2,500' - 7,000'.

Silktassel bush is immediately recognized when its long, silky, drooping catkins are hanging from its branches. The whole plant has a distinctively gray appearance as its elliptic leaves are covered with grayish silky hairs above and more densely below with silky woollike hairs. Even the small (about ½ inch) egg-shaped fruits are densely covered with white silky hairs. Male and female flowers occur on separate plants.

The bush reaches a height of at least 6 feet.

The leaves and twigs have a bitter flavor, but are browsed to some extent by deer, cattle and goats. Because of this bitter taste, it receives the name "quinine-bush."

This genus is sometimes placed in its own family — *Garryaceae* — of which its only member is *Garrya*, containing about 12 species. It is closely related to dogwood.

Wright Silktassel

feverbush, grayleaf "dogwood," "bearberry," "chaparral," "coffee-berry"

Garrya wrightii   Dogwood family *(Cornaceae)*

Range: AZ, NM, w. TX; s. to Mex. Dry slopes, 3,000' - 8,000'.

Wright silktassel differs from the silktassel bush by having only a few small flowers borne in clusters at twig ends, developing into small, hard, dark bluish purple, pea-size fruits. Light green, 1 to 2 inch leaves are long elliptic, leathery and nonsilky which help to differentiate this bush from silktassel bush.

It is usually a shrub of about 2 to 8 feet tall, but can become a small tree to 15 feet.

Some species contain a bitter alkaloid, garryin, which has been used as a tonic and as a preventative for recurring diseases such as malaria. A Mexican species is much used as a remedy for diarrhea.

Silktassel woods are hard and heavy.

Rubber in small quantities has been extracted from this species.

Silver Buffaloberry

bull-, squaw-, or rabbitberry; silverleaf

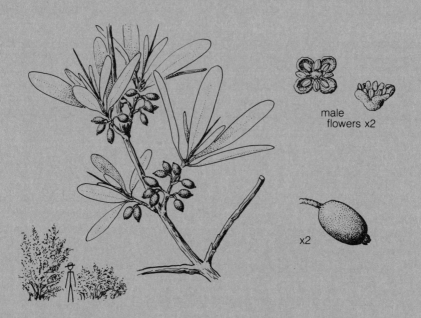

male
flowers x2

x2

Shepherdia argentea

Elaeagnus or Oleaster family
(Elaeagnaceae)

Range: AZ, NM, CO, UT; w. to CA; n. to AK; e. across Can. to Nfld.; ne to ND. Along streams & river bottoms, 3,000' - 7,500'.

A bushy shrub or small tree usually no more than 10 to 15 feet tall, often forming thickets. Its leaves give the name "silver" to it, as they look as if they have been sprayed with silver on both sides. The twigs, too, are silvery gray and often spiny. The gray brown bark shreds into long thin strips.

Male and female flowers are borne on different plants, so that only part of those in a buffaloberry thicket bear fruit (the females). The others (male) produce pollen only. The fruits, produced in profusion, are a bright, glossy scarlet (occasionally golden) with a mealy, tart flesh. The Indians ate them either fresh or dried and stored them for winter use. Early pioneers made a sauce of the berries to garnish buffalo steaks, hence the name buffaloberry. They also put them in stews and mushes for added flavor. The fruits contain a considerable amount of pectin, making them highly suitable for jams, jellies and pies.

Ground squirrels, chipmunks, porcupines and black bear, as well as several species of birds have been known to eat the fruits.

Russian-olive

silvery
and
"warty"
with
tiny stalked
scales

Elaeagnus angustifolia

Elaeagnus or Oleaster family
(Elaeagnaceae)

Range: Our whole range; w. to CA; n. to Can.; s. to Mex. Along streams, 4,500' - 7,000'.

A shrub or small tree native to southern Europe and western Asia, but introduced from Russia as an ornamental shade tree and for windbreaks in arid, windy regions. It has escaped from cultivation and established itself rather widely, mostly in low ground along streams, becoming "naturalized," hence its inclusion here. It grows to about 20 feet tall.

When in the vicinity of a Russian-olive, you might smell it before you see it when it is in full bloom. The small, yellow flowers are unusually fragrant, and their delightful, spicy aroma wafts far from its source.

The most distinguishing features of the Russian-olive, however, are its leaves and fruit, both of which are silvery colored. The miniature olivelike fruits remain on the trees long after the leaves have fallen, providing food for several species of birds throughout the winter and spring.

The fruits, though small and large seeded, can be eaten as they come from the tree. Their flesh is yellow, mealy and somewhat sweet, but pretty tasteless. It has been reported that the fruits can be made into a fair jelly, especially when pectin and sugar are added.

Netleaf Hackberry

sugarberry, false elm, palo blanco

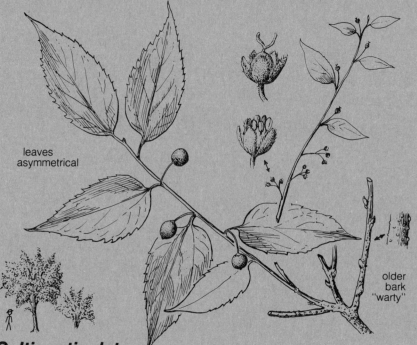

leaves
asymmetrical

older
bark
"warty"

Celtis reticulata   Elm family *(Ulmaceae)*

Range: Our whole range; nw to WA; e. to KS & NB; s. to Mex. Dry, rocky hillsides and canyons, 2,500' - 7,000'.

If you see a tree in the southwest uplands that looks like an elm, but isn't— it's the hackberry, a member of the elm family. American elm comes no closer to our area than the eastern parts of Kansas, Oklahoma and Texas.

Rarely 30 feet high and a foot in diameter, it is more of a large shrub than a tree, sometimes stunted even more when growing in unusually dry places. Bright green, lopsided, saw-toothed, elmlike leaves will also identify it. They turn yellow in the fall just before dropping. The sweet, orange red fruits are pea size and thin pulped but are eaten raw by many Indian tribes. They are considered rather puckery. The fruits, seeds and all, were pounded to a pulp and eaten with fat or mixed with parched corn.

If the Indians or birds don't get them first, the berries sometimes hang on the trees all winter.

The warty bark on the trunks of old trees is distinctive.

Hackberry wood has been used for fenceposts, ax and hoe handles and furniture of a poor grade.

Texas Mulberry

western, dwarf, Mexican, small-leaved or mountain mulberry; moral [the mulberry tree]; baya [berry?]

leaves
rough
to the
touch

Morus microphylla　　　　Mulberry family *(Moraceae)*

Range: c. to se AZ, s. NM, w. TX; s. to Mex. Arroyos and dry slopes, 2,000' - 6,000'.

This mulberry is mostly shrubby, but becomes, under ideal conditions, a scraggly tree seldom over 15 feet tall. In March and April small, inconspicuous, green flowers appear, the males in hanging, many-flowered catkins, and the females in small, few-flowered compact clusters. The small fruits are about ½ inch in size, but may vary somewhat depending on the amount of water the tree receives. These blackberrylike fruits are, at first, red, then dark purple and finally, when ripe in May, black. The ripe fruit is barely palatable (it is rather sour), but when made into pies and jellies is said to be very tasty, possibly because of the added sugar.

Try rubbing the dark green leaves between your fingers. Notice that the upper surfaces of the leaves have a sandpapery feeling.

The Papago and Texas Indians used its wood for making bows and the Havasupai Indians of the Grand Canyon have cultivated this mulberry from time immemorial. Other Indians ate the fruit as well.

In Mexico, the fruits are sometimes seen in the native markets, and Mexican carpenters use the wood to a small extent.

The fruits are quite popular with a number of species of birds and animals, and deer have been known to browse its boughs.

Mulberry is closely related to both elm and nettle; and hemp and marijuana belong to the mulberry family.

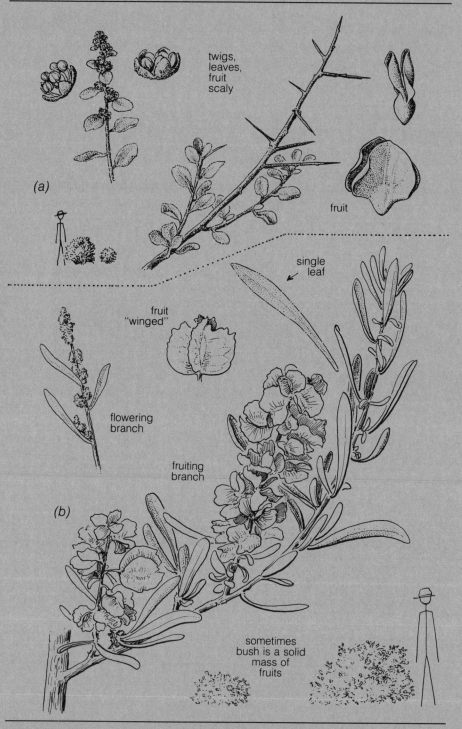

twigs, leaves, fruit scaly

fruit

(a)

single leaf

fruit "winged"

flowering branch

fruiting branch

(b)

sometimes bush is a solid mass of fruits

36

(a) Shadscale

spiny or round-leaf saltbush; sheep-fat

Atriplex confertifolia   Goosefoot family *(Chenopodiaceae)*

Range: Our whole range; w. to CA; n. & nw to MT & OR; ne to ND; s. to Mex. Dry plains & low mesas, 2,500' - 7,500'.

This is another of the nearly 60 species of saltbushes that occur in the United States. A somewhat spiny shrub from 1 to 3 feet tall, its spininess becomes more apparent in winter when the plants become rigid and nearly leafless. Like the four-wing saltbush, its leaf surfaces are silvery gray and scaly, but unlike it, its leaves are rounded and its fruits have two wings instead of four. The wings may vary in color from pale green to a deep rose pink. These are from the female flowers — the male pollen-producing flowers are on separate plants.

Like its relative, four-wing saltbush, its foliage has a salty taste — hence their common name.

Its seeds were used by the Indians of Arizona, Utah and Nevada for making bread and mush.

Where it occurs in nearly pure stands on alkaline soils, it is an important browse plant for cattle, sheep and goats.

(b) Four-wing Saltbush

saltbrush, wingscale, "shadscale," cenizo, chico, chamiza, chamizo

Atriplex canescens   Goosefoot family *(Chenopodiaceae)*

Range: Our whole range; w. to CA; nw to WA, e. to ND & KS; s. to Mex. Dry plains, 2,500' - 8,000'.

Most members of the goosefoot family are regarded as troublesome weeds, as they grow on waste ground and in disturbed places, especially newly plowed fields. Saltbush and greasewood are the shrubby members of this large family. Shadscale, pigweed, tumbleweed and Russian thistle also belong to this family. Russian thistle is a serious pest in this country and is often called Russian tumbleweed. Beets (both garden and sugar) and spinach are cultivated members of this family.

This 2 to 5 foot tall bush has small, gray green, densely branched stems. At summer's end, its tiny, light yellow female flowers (the male flowers are on separate bushes) produce large numbers of conspicuous 4-winged bracts which are light green, papery and quite distinctive. They dry to a pale brown or to nearly white.

Its leaves and young shoots are used as greens, or they can be added to soups. The Indians and Spanish-Americans grind its parched seeds and mix them with sugar and water for a drink called pinole.

It is used extensively — and highly prized — by the Navajos as forage for their cattle, sheep and goats, especially in winter and early spring when other forage is scarce. Other browsers, as deer, pronghorn and rabbits occasionally use it for food. The seeds, too, are eaten by several kinds of birds and small animals. In addition, the shrubby branches provide natural shade and shelter in the relatively open plains for various kinds of wildlife such as quail, horned larks, sparrows, gophers, mice, prairie dogs and kangaroo rats.

For a yellow dye, the Navajo use an infusion of its leaves and twigs.

37

Winter-fat

lamb's-tail, "white sage"

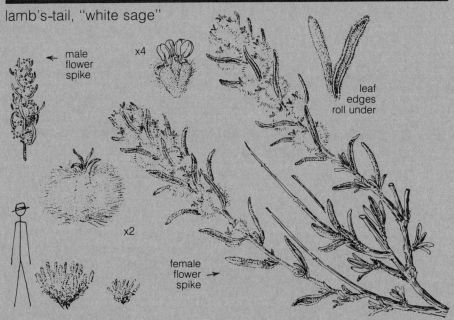

male flower spike

x4

leaf edges roll under

x2

female flower spike

Eurotia lanata   Goosefoot family *(Chenopodiaceae)*

Range: Our whole range; w. to CA; n. to Can.; e. to KS; s. to Mex. Sandy, alkaline soils, 2,500' - 8,000'.

If you come across a cottony-looking low shrub from 1 to 3 feet tall growing in sandy, alkaline soil, it could only be winter-fat.

Its upright, flowering clusters, when gone to seed, fluff out and look like lambs' tails. Although it is not even closely related to the sages, it is sometimes called white, sweet or winter "sage."

Many erect, woolly branches arise from a woody base. Densely hairy, threadlike leaves with rolled-under margins cover the whole plant, giving it a fuzzy, white-hairy appearance. The leaves become dry in the fall but remain on the plant for most of the winter, making it a highly prized forage plant, especially for sheep, when other plants are scarce. Sheep, therefore, can be fattened on it in the winter, giving it its name, "winter-fat." It is reported to have high forage value.

When thoroughly dried, and the long, silvery-silky hairs of the seed heads fluff out, it is used in the home as an attractive dry arrangement, lasting, with care, throughout the winter.

The Navajo parboiled its leaves and ate them to relieve the expectorating of blood. It was thrown on the hot stones of their sweathouses, along with sticky-flowered rabbitbrush for aroma.

Spineless Hop-sage

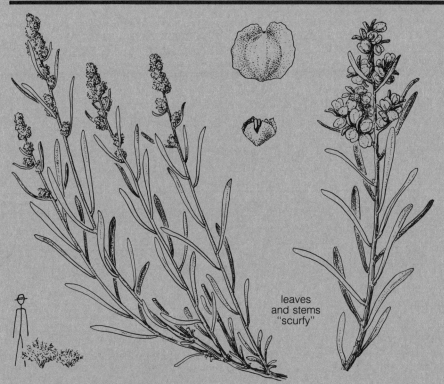

leaves
and stems
"scurfy"

Grayia brandegei   Goosefoot family *(Chenopodiaceae)*

Range: AZ, CO, UT; w. to CA; n. to Can. Dry places, 4,500' - 7,000'.

Another of our shrubs with "sage" in its name, but not related to either true sage or sagebrush; however, its winged fruits do look somewhat like upright hop clusters.

It attains a height of about 2 feet and has stiff spreading branches. The whole plant, its branches, its somewhat fleshy leaves and its fruiting bracts, is mealy looking, especially when young.

Each of its fruits is surrounded by a pair of rounded, papery, pinkish to white wings, crowded together on the branchlet ends, making the plant quite pretty and highly visible when in fruit.

Very similar in general appearance to the saltbush, hop-sage differs, technically, by having its fruiting bract margins wholly joined, while in the saltbushes, the bracts are joined only part way.

Together with winter-fat (opposite), greasewood, saltbush and shadscale, it belongs to the goosefoot family, which includes such cultivated plants as garden and sugar beets as well as spinach.

Black Greasewood

chico, chicobush

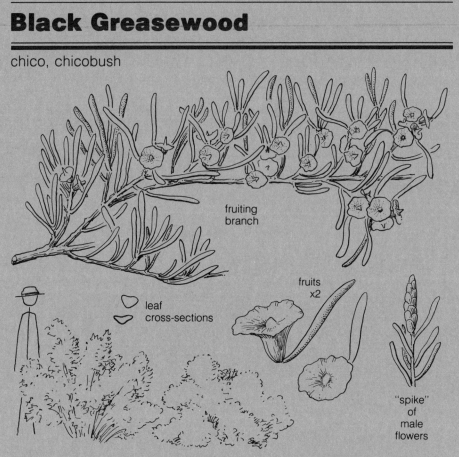

fruiting branch

leaf cross-sections

fruits x2

"spike" of male flowers

Sarcobatus vermiculatus Goosefoot family *(Chenopodiacae)*

Range: Our whole range; w. to CA; n. to Can.; e. across U.S. & Can. to ND & Sask.; s. to Mex. Flat, usually alkaline ground, 2,000' - 8,500'.

A coarse, scraggly, much-branched shrub from 2 to occasionally 8 feet tall, greasewood is readily identified by its narrow, fleshy leaves, its gray-, whitish- or tan-colored bark and its spreading rigid branches. The succulent pale green leaves are salty tasting and were used by the Indians as greens. They also ate its seeds.

The male flowers appear in catkinlike spikes at branch ends, whereas the usually solitary female flowers occur in the leaf axils to become seeds surrounded by a green to tan membranous wing, sometimes tinged with red.

Pronghorn, prairie dogs and California quail make minor use of greasewood for food, but for the jackrabbit it is a major food source. Its low-to-the-ground rigid branches give excellent protective covering to small animals as well as shade from the heat of day.

Greasebush

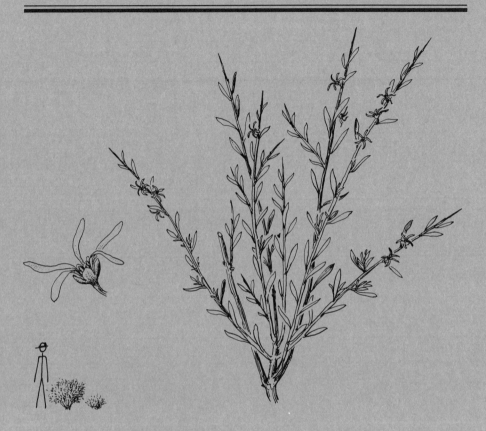

Glossopetalon spinescens Bittersweet family *(Celastraceae)*

Range: Our whole range; w. to CA; n. to WA; s. to Mex. Dry hills and desert canyons, 4,500' - 5,500'.

A spiny, olive green stemmed dwarf shrub scattered throughout our range. It is mostly 1 to 2 feet tall, occurring from the upper margins of the desert through the pinyon-juniper woodlands. Tiny, deciduous pale green leaves up to ½ inch long cover the seemingly disorderly array of angled branches. The white flowers are even tinier — no more than about ⅜ of an inch long, bursting forth from the juncture of the leaves with the stem.

The only other plant included in the book that belongs to this family is mountain lover in the fir-aspen belt. Burningbush belongs to this family which also has been called burningbush family and stafftree family. The family is closely related to the sumac and maple families.

Even though the plant is spiny, it is browsed by deer and sheep.

Yuccas

Spanish bayonets, Spanish daggers, Adam's needles, Our Lord's candles, amoles, dátiles [dates], jaboncillas [little soap (plants)], palmillas [little palm trees], yucas

Lily family *(Liliaceae)*

Yuccas are pollinated by the yucca moth — an example of interdependence, since the moth cannot reproduce without yuccas (eggs are laid during pollination and the larvae feed upon the seeds).

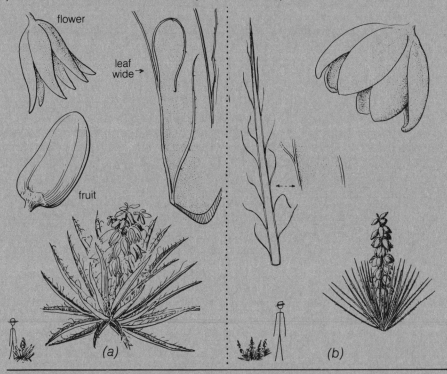

Banana Yucca *(a)*   Indian banana, blue yucca, dátil   *Yucca baccata*
Range: Our whole range; w. to CA. Dry plains & slopes, 4,500' - 8,000'.
   This species has a fat, bananalike fruit and broad, stiff leaves.
   Various Indian tribes ate the ripe, fleshy fruit either fresh or cooked. If the unripe fruit was used, it was first roasted. For later use it was roasted, ground, pressed into cakes and sun dried. The seeds as well as the flower buds were also roasted and eaten.

Navajo Yucca *(b)*   *Yucca navajoa*
Range: AZ, NM, CO, UT; w. to NV. Sandy & rocky places, 4,500' - 7,500'.
   A low, densely clumped yucca with leathery, white-margined leaves.
   It forms clumps of about 10 rosettes (but this varies from 1 to 44). It is easy to confuse this species with Great Plains yucca.

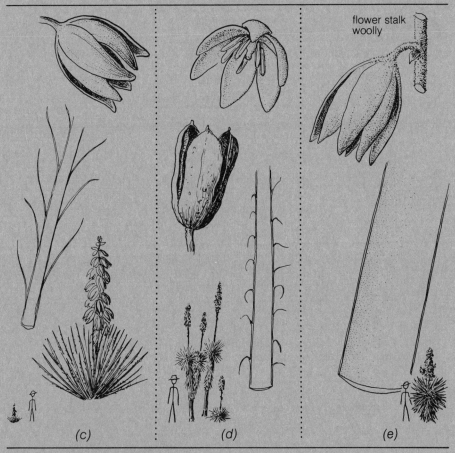

flower stalk woolly

(c)   *(d)*   *(e)*

Narrowleaf Yucca *(c)*   fineleaf yucca   ***Yucca angustissima***

Range: AZ, NM, CO, UT; w. to NV. Dry mesas & slopes, 2,700' - 7,500'. This species has dry, erect seed pods and very narrow leaves.

It is usually stemless, but sometimes has short stems that lie on the ground. As with other yuccas, its fruits were eaten raw, roasted or dried for winter.

Soaptree Yucca *(d)*   soapweed yucca   ***Yucca elata***

Range: AZ, NM, w. TX; s. to Mex. Dry, sandy places, 1,500' - 6,000'. A slender-leaved yucca with a definite trunk 6 to 15 feet tall.

It is the State flower of New Mexico. Both the Pima and Papago use the leaves in basket making. The young stalks which look somewhat like overgrown asparagus were eaten.

Schotts Yucca *(e)*   mountain yucca, hoary yucca   ***Yucca schottii***

Range: se AZ, sw NM; s. to Mex. Hillsides & canyon slopes, 4,000' - 7,000'. A treelike yucca with nonshredding leaf margins. It grows from 6 to 20 feet tall, with a trunk diameter of 8 to 12 inches. Its fleshy fruit was eaten in Arizona.

43

Smooth Bouvardia

Bouvardia glaberrima

Madder family *(Rubiaceae)*

Range: s. AZ, s. NM; s. to Mex. Dry, shady slopes and in canyons, 3,000' - 9,000'.

This and the buttonbush (opposite), belong to the large, mostly tropical family which includes both coffee and quinine trees.

Smooth bouvardia is a low shrub, attaining a height of only 2 or 3 feet, with bark that is pale at first but turning brownish later. It grows on dry, partially shaded hillsides and canyonsides. Its narrow, tapered leaves are distinctively arranged around the stem, mostly in whorls of 3s, but occasionally in 2s or 4s.

Bright red to pink, or sometimes white, flowers appear clustered at the tips of the branches from May to October and resemble honeysuckle flowers, a plant to which it is closely related. The flowers are narrow and trumpetlike and about 1 inch long with their throats flaring into 4 lobes.

The genus has about 30 species that are grown in greenhouses outside of tropical America. It is such a handsome shrub that it has often been suggested as worthy of being planted outside as an ornamental where the weather is semitropical.

In Mexico it is said to be "good for" such diverse ailments as hydrophobia and dysentery.

Buttonbush

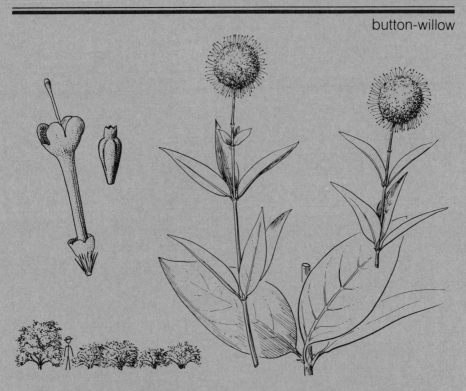

Cephalanthus occidentalis   Madder family *(Rubiaceae)*

Range: s. AZ, s. NM, w. TX; w. to CA; from the midwest to Can. & Atl. Coast; s. to Mex. & W. Indies; also in e. Asia. Swampy places and along streams, 1,000' - 6,000'.

In our range, the buttonbush is a large shrub from 6 to 8 (or 12) feet tall with a trunk as thick, sometimes, as 1 foot. It often forms thickets in swamps and along streams. Our species is one of only 6 to 8 species in the world. Young branches are reddish brown, but eventually turn a gray brown color. Leaves are dark green and smooth above and somewhat hairy and lighter beneath. They are arranged opposite each other or in groups of threes. Its minute, fragrant white flowers are packed in dense spherical heads, or "buttons" about an inch in diameter, reminding one of sycamore buttons.

In the treatment of bronchial troubles and skin and venereal diseases, its bark has been used medicinally. Bees are attracted to its flowers, and waterfowl feed on the seeds.

Because of its attractive foliage and flower heads, buttonbush is sometimes planted as an ornamental.

45

Boxelder

ashleaf maple, boxelder maple, maple-ash

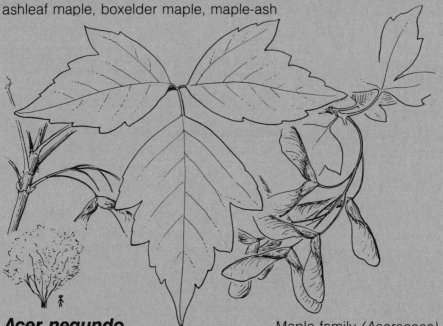

Acer negundo   Maple family *(Aceraceae)*

Range: Our whole range; w. to CA; n. to Can.; e. to Atl. Coast; s. to Mex. Streambanks and moist land, 3,500' - 8,500'.

This tree is neither a boxwood nor an elder, but a maple. It may take its name from its white wood which resembles that of the boxwood shrub and from its elderlike leaves. It was sometimes "boxed" (tapped) for its sweet sap — another possible origin for its name.

A medium-size, freely branching tree about 50 feet in height, but more often than not it is a many-stemmed shrub of 10 to 15 feet.

The double-winged seeds identify it as a maple; however, its leaves are very un-maple-like, being divided into 3 (sometimes 5) coarsely toothed leaflets (p. 95). Its bark is greenish and smooth on new twigs, but pale grayish brown and cracked on old trunks. Because of the brittleness of its wood, it is subject to damage during wind and snowstorms. When fall arrives, the leaves turn a pale yellow, adding yet another autumnal color to the varied landscape.

Boxelder has often been planted as a shade tree because of its rapid growth, and because of this, it becomes "naturalized" where it has escaped from cultivation. Unfortunately it is short-lived. It was first cultivated in 1688.

In areas where sugar maple does not grow, both Indians and white men tapped the boxelder for its sweetish sap to make syrup and sugar, both inferior to the "real" maple syrup made from the sugar maple tree.

Arizona Sycamore

Arizona planetree, buttonball tree, buttonwood, ciclamor, "álamo"

Platanus wrightii Sycamore or Planetree family *(Platanaceae)*

Range: c. to se AZ, sw NM; s. to Mex. Streams & lakesides, 2,000' - 7,000'.

Once you've seen a sycamore, you'll never forget it. Its striking features are mottled bark, large maplelike leaves and swinging "buttonballs." The mottled effect is caused by its loose, thin, brownish bark flaking away and exposing patches of whitish to pale green inner bark.

The tree grows to 80 feet with a trunk diameter of 4 feet, but is occasionally a sprawling, spread-out tree, divided at the ground into 2 or 3 large stems, some of which may even repose on the ground.

Innumerable seeds are densely packed into dry brownish "buttonballs" which remain on the trees until spring when they separate and the downy tufts attached to the seeds waft them into the breezes.

The "sycamore" of the Bible is not related, but a kind of fig tree.

Bush Mint

mint bush, hoary rosemary-mint

Poliomintha incana

Mint family *(Labiatae)*

Range: Our whole range; w. to CA; s. to Mex. Dry, sunny, sandy sites, 4,000' - 6,000'.

If you should see a medium-size shrub in the distance that looks as if it were covered with hoar frost, it is probably bush mint. The entire plant — leaves, young stems, sepals — is clothed in a silvery white coat of minute feltlike hairs. All in all a very attractive plant. It responds well to cultivation. In our range this mint grows not over 3 feet high and is very aromatic.

Typical mint flowers with lower and upper lips arise from the leaf axils, either singly or in clusters of 2 or 3. The pale blue to pale purple flowers begin to appear as early as April and continue to bloom into September. Occasionally the flowers are white with purple dots on their lower lips.

It has been reported that the Hopi eat the leaves raw or boiled, sometimes dipping them in salt. They were also dried for winter use. Even the flowers were used for seasoning foods.

Other members of the mint family which all contain aromatic oils used in flavoring and cookery are: basil, horehound, marjoram, mint, orégano, sage, savory, spearmint and thyme.

Yerba (Hierba) Santa

mountain-balm

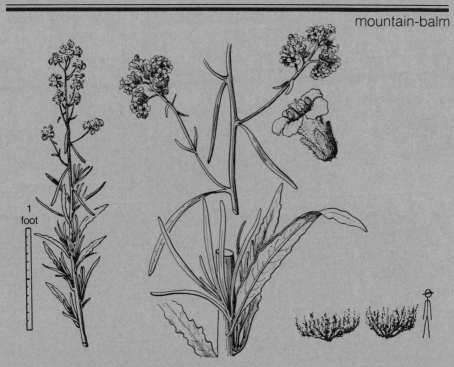

Eriodictyon angustifolium

Waterleaf family
(Hydrophyllaceae)

Range: AZ, s. UT; w. to CA. Dry slopes, 2,000' - 7,000'.

An aromatic, evergreen shrub growing to no more than 4 feet tall. Pale lilac-colored (sometimes whitish) little bells hang gracefully in clusters which are curled up at the ends like scorpion tails, uncurling as the flowers develop.

Its leathery leaves are simple, with toothed margins that are slightly turned back. They are dark green and sticky above, and densely white woolly beneath, between the network of veins. The leaves as well as the branches and twigs exude a sticky, aromatic substance.

Most plants that emit strong aromas "naturally must be good for something." Yerba santa is no exception: It is considered to be very useful in allaying coughs and the attendant sore throats. The name itself indicates that it is an herb with supernatural powers.

Up to 2 percent of the mule deers' diet consists of this plant.

Besides yerba santa, baby blue-eyes, California blue-bell, purple fringe, scorpionweed, whispering bells and wild-heliotrope belong to the waterleaf family.

New Mexican Forestiera

New Mexico olive, desert olive, wild or mountain privet, adelia, palo blanco, "ironwood"

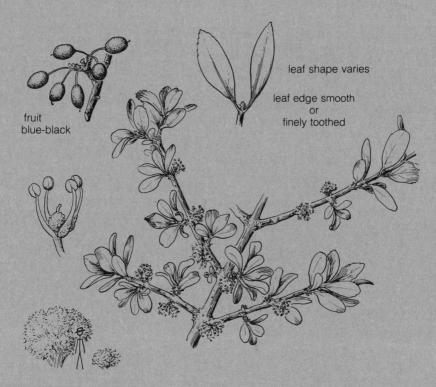

fruit
blue-black

leaf shape varies

leaf edge smooth
or
finely toothed

Forestiera neomexicana

Olive family *(Oleaceae)*

Range: Our whole range; w. to CA. River valleys & cliff bases, 3,000' - 7,000'.

Typically, an erect, spreading shrub (rarely a small tree) from 3 to 10 feet tall, with spiny branches sometimes. Its small and inconspicuous flowers have no petals and the male and female flowers are separate entities, with the stamens giving the flowers a yellowish cast. The leaves which are grayish green and oval appear after the blossoms. Small, bluish black, olive-shaped fruits ripen and drop from the trees in late summer and fall.

New Mexican forestiera is another shrub that has a very hard wood, and like many others, is called "ironwood." Because of this hardness, made even more so by fire-hardening, the Hopi Indians made digging sticks of its wood. Its wood (palo) is white (blanco).

The Navajo used its wood for making prayersticks of the South, possibly because the small fruits are blue, the "color" of South.

Yellow Menodora

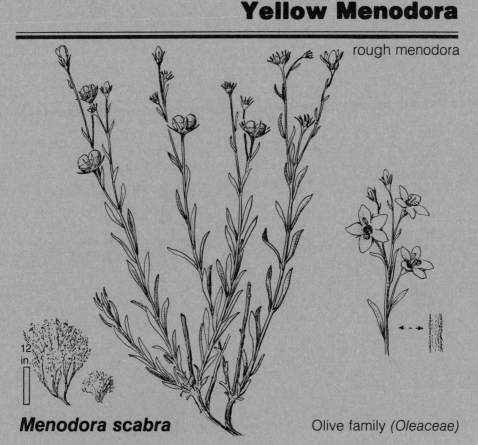

Menodora scabra   Olive family *(Oleaceae)*

Range: Our whole range; w. to CA; s. to Mex. Dry, rocky slopes, 1,500' - 7,500'.

A small, deciduous, somewhat twiggy, subshrub with thick, rough, dull green leaves, growing only about 2 feet tall. The flowers are bright yellow, funnel shaped and rather showy, and appear in open clusters at twig ends. The bush starts blooming in May and continues into August, producing inflated, twin-sphered, dry capsules in the fall. The dry capsule differentiates it from the New Mexican forestiera (opposite) which has a fleshy, olivelike fruit.

Menodora belongs to the olive family, along with New Mexican forestiera and the ashes. The family also includes such seemingly unrelated cultivated plants as privets, lilacs, jasmines and forsythias.

Animals browse it nearly everywhere it grows, but it doesn't seem to be too important as a browse plant.

The Navajo consider it "their plant."

The plant was first described in 1852 by Asa Gray, an authority on western plants, from a specimen collected in 1846 by Dr. Frederick Augustus Wislizenius, a German-born naturalist of St. Louis.

51

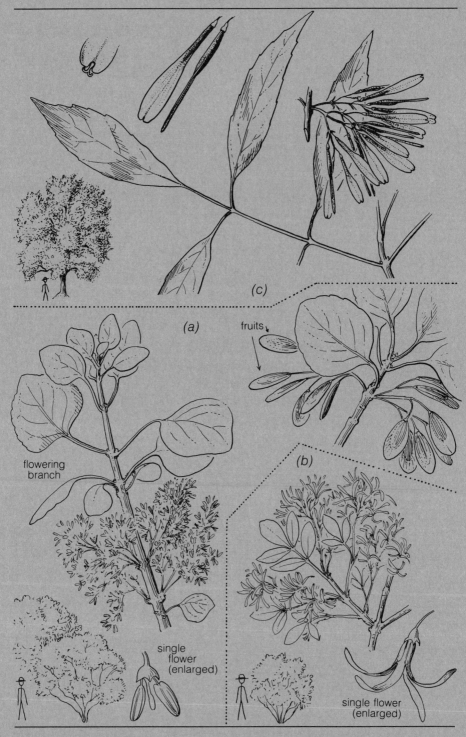

(a)

(c)

fruits

flowering
branch

single
flower
(enlarged)

(b)

single flower
(enlarged)

Singleleaf Ash (a)   dwarf ash, fresno

Fraxinus anomala   Olive family *(Oleaceae)*

Range: n. AZ, nw NM, sw CO, s. UT. Canyons & hillsides, 2,000' - 6,000'.

This ash is a shrubby tree seldom exceeding 20 feet in height and a trunk diameter of 6 inches. Its twigs are 4-angled and slightly winged, orange colored at first, later round and ashy gray.

Unlike our other ash trees which have 3 to 7 leaflets per leaf, this ash has only a single leaf (rarely 2 or 3 leaflets). These nearly round, thickish leaves are dark green above, paler below and hairy underneath when young. Because of the absence of petals, and the presence of sepals only, the flowers are pale green. They develop into small clusters of single, wing-margined, maplelike fruits (keys).

Early settlers found that its tough wood made good tool handles.

This ash seems to be of only moderate importance to wildlife; however, a number of birds and animals eat the seeds. Deer browse the foliage.

Fragrant Ash (b)   flowering ash, fresno

Fraxinus cuspidata var. *macropetala*

Range: AZ, NM, w. TX; s. to Mex. Rocky slopes, 3,500' - 5,500'.

This ash is unique among our ashes — its flowers have petals and are fragrant. It is a shrub or low tree, growing to about 20 feet tall, sometimes forming thickets. After its white blooms fade, one-seeded, pale green fruits with conspicuous wings appear and hang in drooping clusters.

Its leaves have 5 to 7 leaflets, in contrast to the singleleaf ash, and are dark green above and lighter green beneath.

The young twigs shade from gray green to brown, but as they grow older, tend to turn gray.

Velvet Ash (c)   Arizona, desert or smooth ash; fresno

Fraxinus velutina

Range: AZ, sw NM, sw UT, w. TX; w. to CA; s. to Mex. Canyon bottoms, 2,000' - 7,000'.

Velvety-surfaced young leaves distinguish this ash from the other two, but the velvet from the upper side of the leaf is not for long — it soon wears off.

This is the largest of our three ashes. It can grow to tree size of 50 feet with a trunk diameter of 18 inches, but in our range, it is generally about half this size. It has 3 to 7 leaflets per leaf. They are green above and paler beneath.

Velvet ash is moderately used as food by birds and animals who usually peel off the wing before eating the attached seeds.

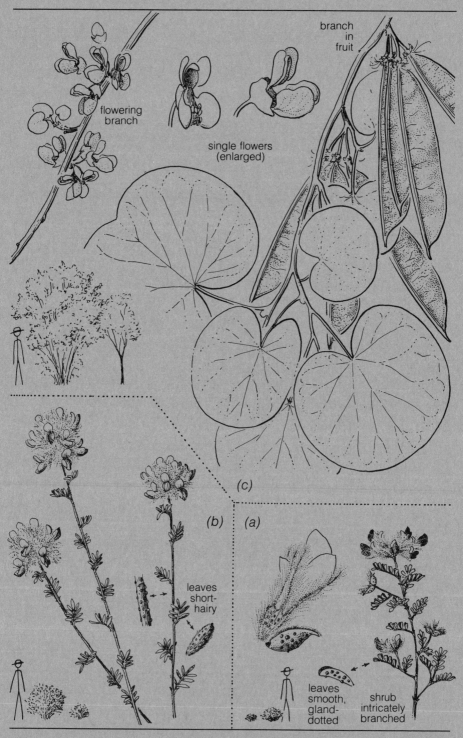

flowering branch

single flowers (enlarged)

branch in fruit

(c)

(b)

(a)

leaves short-hairy

leaves smooth, gland-dotted

shrub intricately branched

(a) Feather Dalea

indigobush

Dalea formosa
Pea family *(Leguminosae)*

Range: Our whole range; s. to Mex. Dry plains & low hills, 2,000' - 6,500'.

The species name of this dalea is *formosa* (beautiful), and true to this name, it is indeed a handsome bush with large and showy rose purple to indigo, sweet-pea-like flowers 2 to 6 in a cluster. They appear from March to June and sometimes again in September. It is a low shrub, under 3 feet tall, but much branched with rigid, light gray twigs which are pointed, sometimes spinelike. Its leaves are divided into 7 or 9 (occasionally up to 15) leaflets.

Its more famous cousin is the smoke tree of the deserts.

It is especially savored by deer, and kangaroo rats eat the seeds.

(b) Wislizenius Dalea

Dalea wislizenii
Pea family *(Leguminosae)*

Range: Limited to se AZ & sw NM; s. to Mex. Rocky hillsides, 3,000' - 6,000'.

Very similar to feather dalea, differing mostly in that the leaflets and twigs are hairy and the blooms are in many-flowered spikes instead of few-flowered clusters. Kangaroo rats eat it.

(c) California Redbud

Arizona or western redbud; Judas tree; árbol de Judas; bóton encarnado [red bud]

Cercis occidentalis
Pea family *(Leguminosae)*

Range: nw AZ, s. & sw UT, w. TX; w. to CA. Rocky hillsides & canyons, 4,000' - 6,000'.

California redbud burgeons in early spring, covering itself with myriad, showy, purplish pink, pealike flowers (p. 93) which appear before the leaves, even bursting forth from the trunk — a sight not soon forgotten. Pale green, flattened, pealike pods follow the flowers, but soon turn brownish, to dangle from the branches all winter. Its kidney-shaped leaves turn yellowish before dropping off.

The Navajo roasted the pods, ate the seeds and made an incense from the leaves for the Mountain Chant. Many other Indian tribes used the twigs of redbud in basketry. Split twigs with the bark left on were used to make patterns.

The Judas tree, according to legend, was the tree from which Judas hanged himself, and the flowers, white at the time, turned color with shame and have blushed ever since. (It is also claimed that the tree was an elderberry.)

False-indigo

indigobush, bastard indigo

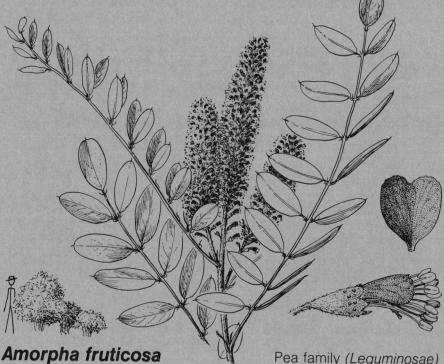

Amorpha fruticosa   Pea family *(Leguminosae)*

Range: AZ, NM, CO, w. TX; w. to CA; ne to Sask. & New Eng.; e. to FL. Moist places, 2,500' - 6,000'.

Although false-indigo is a member of the pea family, its flowers are not pealike, nor do they resemble any other flower, for they have only one petal, the other four being absent.

It is a relatively tall shrub of variable size from 4 to 10 (sometimes 18) feet tall. It grows in dense stands almost anywhere that there is the least bit of moisture: streambanks, irrigation ditches, swamp borders, pastures, gullies and on the edges of woods.

The pretty little violet purple florets grow in long, dense, spikelike clusters at the ends of the branches, and bloom from May to July. Its leaves are locustlike and have from 11 to 15 (sometimes more) leaflets per stem. They turn yellow in the fall just before dropping. It is sometimes planted as an ornamental shrub.

The Kiowa Indians used its branches for temporary bedding, and the Pawnee spread the plants on the ground to keep freshly butchered meat clean, possibly because it was the handiest plant available.

flowers have
no petals

Parryella filifolia

Pea family *(Leguminosae)*

Range: n. AZ, n. NM, sw CO only. Dry, often sandy, hills, 4,000' - 6,000'.

Dunebroom is a low, much-branched, shrubby plant growing about 2 to 3 feet high, with slender, broomlike twigs and very slender glandular-dotted leaflets. Its flowers are very small and dull yellowish or yellowish green and composed of sepals — the petals are entirely absent. They occur in loose, spikelike racemes up to 6 inches long, at branch ends. Old twigs are brown or ashy gray, but when younger are greenish to reddish brown. The whole bush is slightly aromatic.

The Hopi use the twigs in making baskets and brooms; the seeds in helping to alleviate toothache; and the leaves to kill insects.

Dunebroom receives its name not only because of its broomlike aspect, but also because it occurs in sandy places where it catches the blowing sand and forms miniature sand dunes. Because dunebroom is so well adapted to growing in these places, it is sometimes planted to reduce wind erosion.

Tomatillo

pale lycium, pale wolfberry; desert-, rabbit-, box- or squawthorn; matrimony vine; chico, cambronera [thornylike], tomatilla

Lycium pallidum   Nightshade or Potato family *(Solanaceae)*

Range: Our whole range; w. to CA; s. to Mex. Dry plains & hills, 3,500' - 7,000'.

One of the most useful small shrubs of our area and used by man throughout the Southwest, accounting for its numerous popular names. Livestock, birds and other animals make use of it for food, (berries, browse) and other purposes (retreats, roosts).

Easily identified when in fruit by its tomato-shaped and tomato-colored, marble-size fruits [Sp.: tomatillo(a) (little tomato)]. It belongs to the same family as our garden variety of tomato. The white or "Irish" potato, eggplant, cayenne and chili peppers also belong to this family, as well as such other diverse plants as tobacco, petunia and belladonna.

This medium-size, somewhat spiny shrub reaches a height of 6 feet, but averages closer to about 3 feet. Pale gray green leaves are clustered around short spines, and the showy flowers hang like so many small yellowish green trumpets (sometimes tinged with lavender) from the leaf clusters.

In the Southwest, the Indians eat the fruits as they come off the bush, occasionally with clay to prevent the griping pains resulting from eating too many or eating partially ripe fruits. The clay acts as an "extender" in times of critical shortages as well as helping to take the edge off the fruit's bitter taste.

The berries were also boiled "to just the right consistency" and spread on rocks to dry in the sun, after which they were stored for future use, usually to be reconstituted into soup or sauce, but occasionally they were nibbled on in the dry state.

Cholla

cane, walkingstick, shrub, tree, candelabrum cactus; velas de coyote [coyote candles], cardenche

fruit yellow, not spiny

flowers magenta

Opuntia imbricata

Cactus family *(Cactaceae)*

Range: AZ, NM, UT, w. TX; s. to Mex. Dry plains & hillsides, 4,000' - 7,500'.

This cholla usually grows to 6 feet high, but in favorable locations it will grow up to 15 feet tall with a trunk diameter to 10 inches, qualifying it as a small "tree." Its trunk is short, but soon branches and rebranches into erect candelabrumlike stems.

Red purple (occasionally rose pink) flowers from 2 to 3 inches broad appear in early summer. Dry, yellow, lumpy fruits follow, and, at a distance, are often mistaken for flowers. They remain on the plants all winter. It has been reported that the fruits were eaten either raw or cooked by the Indians of Arizona and New Mexico.

The spiny branches provide protected nesting sites for birds, especially the cactus wren. During Holy Week processions, "Penitentes" bound the spiny branches to their naked backs as an act of contrition.

When the plants die, hollow, cylindrical cores remain, consisting of diamond-shaped holes surrounded by a woody network. These are often made into walkingsticks (hence one of its names), or used for ornamental curios as picture frames, lamps, furniture, etc.

Blackbrush(-bush)

"burrobrush(-bush)"

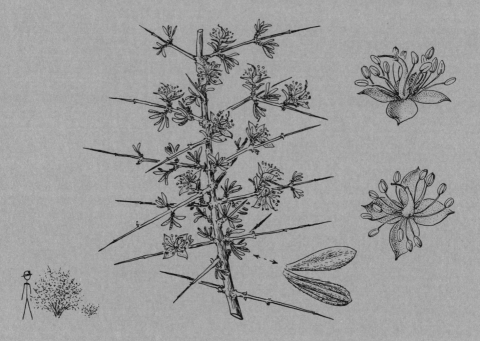

Coleogyne ramosissima Rose family *(Rosaceae)*

Range: AZ, NM, CO, UT; w. to CA. Dry, rocky ground, 3,000' - 6,500'.

Blackbrush receives its name from the dark gray of the twigs which turn blackish with age, and even darker when wet by infrequent rains.

It differs from mountain-mahogany: its petal-like sepals have 4 instead of 5 lobes, its branches often end in spinelike tips, and the fruits have no long tails. Its flowers are small, though showy (about ½ inch across), yellowish (sometimes greenish or purple tinged) and solitary, lasting but a few days.

Its ½ inch leaves are thickish, have rolled-under edges and are somewhat crowded in bundles.

Six feet is its maximum height, while the mountain-mahogany is somewhat taller. This dense, low-growing and wide-spreading, typically desert shrub creeps upward into the pinyon-juniper belt.

It is eaten to a limited extent by wildlife and domestic stock, especially sheep and goats. It can withstand relatively heavy browsing by animals.

Fernbush

portion
of leaf
x4

both glandular
hairs
and starlike

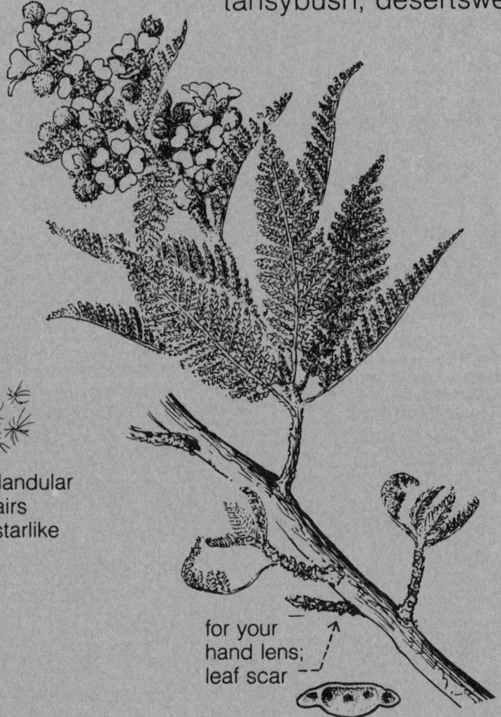

for your
hand lens;
leaf scar

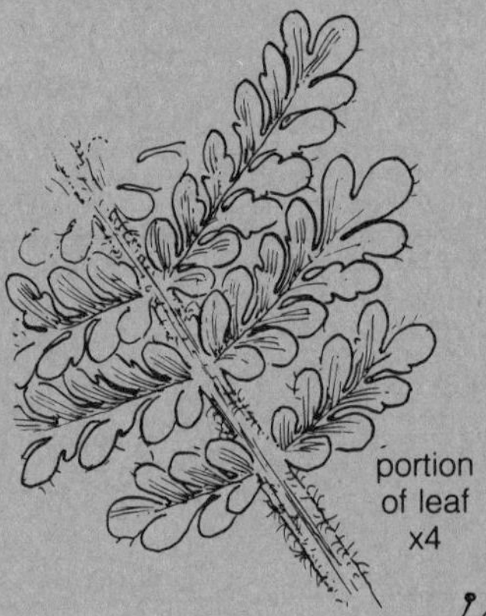

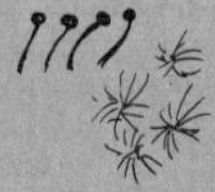

Chamaebatiaria millefolium   Rose family *(Rosaceae)*

Range: AZ, CO (?), UT; w. to CA; nw to OR; n. to WY. Rocky places, 4,000' - 7,000'

Small, fernlike leaves — or tansylike leaves if you are familiar with the garden tansy — should immediately identify this shrub. And if that is not enough "touch and smell" will tell: the leaves are very finely divided and fuzzy-sticky and emit a delightful aromatic fragrance.

Although the white, crinkly petalled flowers are only about ½ inch across, they burst forth in large branching clusters in such profusion that the bushes are very showy from mid- to late summer during the blooming season. The blooms resemble those of the apple, also a member of the rose family.

A low, dense shrub, from about 2½ to 5 feet high, it has a bark that is shreddy and reddish tinged.

For some reason, cattle seem to avoid the fernbush, but deer, sheep and goats browse upon its stems and leaves.

So much do the flowers resemble those of the spiraeas that, when first discovered in 1857, the plant was described as such.

61

Alderleaf Mountain-mahogany

featherbush, hard tack, palo duro

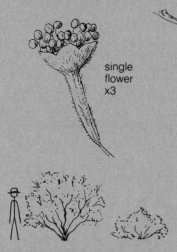

single
flower
x3

Cercocarpus montanus

Rose family *(Rosaceae)*

Range: Our whole range; w. to NV; n. to OR & MT; e. to KS; s. to Mex. Dry slopes & mesas, 3,000' - 9,500'.

This shrub covers many a dry, sunny mesa slope in this belt, growing generally from 4 to 6 feet tall, but sometimes 12 to 20 feet. Its leaves are rather small, wedge shaped and toothed only on the upper margins. The flowers, if they can be called that, burst forth in May and sometimes continue into November. As with all mountain-mahoganies, the flower petals are absent, but the sepals form a small, inconspicuous greenish tube with flared, pinkish to reddish, petallike lobes rimming its mouth.

The 1½ to 3 inch long fuzzy, spirally twisted tails on the small fruits make the plant very conspicuous in the fall and on into winter. Its wood, although difficult to hack with an ax, is brittle and breaks readily. Seasoned wood furnishes excellent firewood.

The Spanish name palo duro means hard wood. The Navajo name signifies a plant "whose wood is as heavy as stone." They use its wood, because of its hardness, as staffs to hold wool when spinning it. The Navajo also used this shrub in preparing a reddish dye for wool. It was made by combining mountain-mahogany with the powdered bark of the alder, to which was added juniper bark; the whole mixture was then steeped. Dice were made from it, and prayersticks of the East were made of its wood, probably because its silky, tailed fruits were white, the "color" of East. Its root and bark were used as a stomachic.

Many wild animals as well as domestic livestock browse the twigs and leaves, to which elk and deer show a preference.

Birchleaf Mountain-mahogany

birchleaf cercocarpus, hard tack, ironwood, sweetbrush

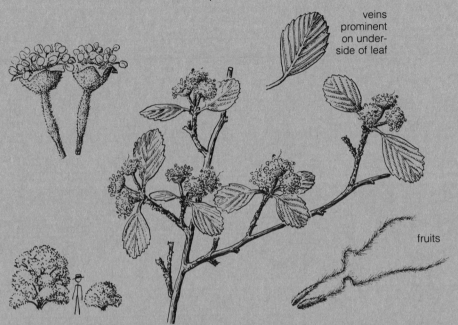

veins prominent on under- side of leaf

fruits

Cercocarpus betuloides

Rose family *(Rosaceae)*

Range: AZ; w. to CA; n. to OR; s. to Mex. Dry slopes, 3,000' - 6,500'.

In our range, this mountain-mahogany is an erect shrub which grows to about 8 feet, or occasionally treelike to 20 feet. It differs basically from alderleaf mountain-mahogany (opposite) whose leaves are sparingly gray silky above in contrast to those of this species which are dark green and smooth above. None of the mountain-mahoganies have petals, but have modified calyx lobes that look like petals.

"Ironwood" is a catch-all name for any shrub whose wood is "as hard as iron," and birchleaf mountain-mahogany is no exception. Its wood is exceptionally hard and heavy, and when green will sink in water. "Hard tack" is given to it for the same reason, and although the origin of "tack" is cloudy, it probably means "food." "Sweetbrush" is used because browsers such as deer, pronghorn and elk, as well as sheep, goats and cattle seem to like its "sweetness." Grouse eat its seeds and leaves.

The mountain-mahoganies are members of the economically important rose family that includes many of our very important fruit-producing plants such as almond, apple, apricot, blackberry, cherry, peach, pear, raspberry and strawberry.

Cliffrose

Stansbury cliffrose, quinine-bush, "buckbrush"

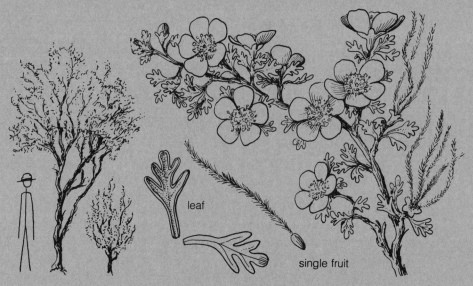

leaf

single fruit

Cowania stansburiana

Rose family *(Rosaceae)*

Range: Our whole range; w. to CA; s. to Mex. Dry slopes, 3,000' - 8,000'.

Cliffrose and Apache-plume (opposite) are closely related shrubs and are similar in appearance. Basic differences are: cliffrose has glandular-dotted leaves, usually 5 feathery plumes per cluster and cream-colored flowers, (p. 95). Apache-plume's leaves are without dots, its feathery plumes are numerous (up to 25) and the flowers are white. Apache-plume grows to 25 feet high; cliffrose only to 6 feet.

When covered with cream-colored, roselike flowers in early summer, cliffrose is a handsome little shrub; and come fall, it is covered with clematislike feathery tails, continuing its loveliness.

Several Indian tribes used cliffrose for various purposes:

Navajo: shredded bark for padding cradleboards (it is very absorbent) and for stuffing pillows and "baseballs;" wood for "female" prayersticks ("male" prayersticks, from mountain-mahogany); leaves and stems mixed with pounded juniper branches for a yellow brown or tan dye; and its straight branches for ceremonial arrows.

Hopi: leaves and twigs to induce vomiting and as a cleansing (and therefore, healing) agent for sores and wounds; wood for arrows.

Basketmakers: clothing, mats, rope and sandals from shredded bark.

The leaves are very bitter tasting (to us), hence the name "quinine-bush," but deer and livestock nibble them when in dire need.

Apache-plume

feather-rose, feather duster bush, poñil

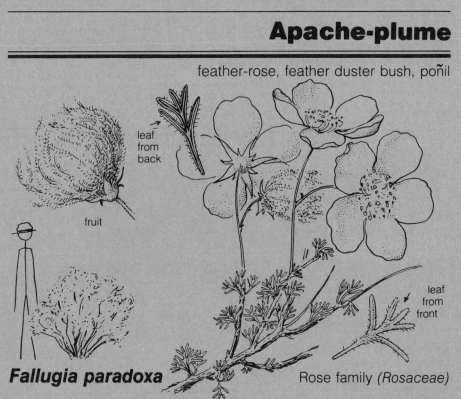

leaf from back

fruit

leaf from front

Fallugia paradoxa Rose family *(Rosaceae)*

Range: Our whole range; w. to CA; s. to Mex. Dry, rocky slopes and washes, 3,500' - 8,000'.

White, solitary flowers as large as apple blossoms appear in abundance from June to August, followed by clusters of feathery-tailed fruits, at first greenish, later tinged with red. They remain on the plant for some time and are every bit as beautiful, in their own way, as the flowers. The blossoms resemble single, white roses or thimbleberry blooms, and indicate that it is a member of the rose family.

Apache-plume is a more striking plant when in fruit than cliffrose (opposite), mostly because it has up to five times as many feathery plumes in each cluster. The cluster so resembles a miniature old-fashioned feather duster, that it has become one of its common names.

Its most common name "Apache-plume" derives from the fact that the fuzzy clusters look like Indian feather war bonnets (war bonnets are a Plains Indian invention, but the plant grows in Apache country).

Its slender branches are whitish, soon becoming shaggy or shreddy.

The stems were used by some Indians for arrows and brooms, while others made a brew from the leaves to promote hair growth.

The shrub is not heavily browsed, but deer, as well as cattle, goats and sheep eat it, and it becomes a more valuable winter forage when other browse becomes scarce.

Mockorange

"syringa," jeringuilla [little syringa]

leaf shape
variable

Philadelphus microphyllus Saxifrage family *(Saxifragaceae)*

Range: Our whole range; w. to CA; n. to WY; s. to Mex. Dry, rocky slopes, 4,000' - 8,000'.

Mockorange flowers are delightfully fragrant, and remind some people of the sweet smell of orange blossoms, giving the shrub its common name; yet others will say that it has a pineapplelike fragrance. It is commonly called "syringa," but the name is usually reserved for the lilacs of the olive family.

It is an erect shrub, normally growing only about 4 feet tall, with peeling, shreddy bark of a reddish brown or tan shade. The numerous, small, narrow leaves, an inch or so long, are slightly glossy and green above, but downy and paler underneath. The large, attractive, 4-petalled, white flowers are showy and fragrant, and bloom from June to August.

The stems were used by the Indians for bows and arrows as well as for pipe stems. Indians of New Mexico ate the fruits, or so it has been reported.

It seems to be of little import in the diet of wildlife, and only the bighorn sheep have been reported as browsing it.

This species closely resembles the mockoranges that are planted as ornamental shrubs. The cultivated variety is a different species imported from southern Europe; however, our species may have been the one exported to France years ago to help breed hardiness into the not-so-hardy European species.

The Lewis mockorange is the State flower of Idaho.

False Mockorange

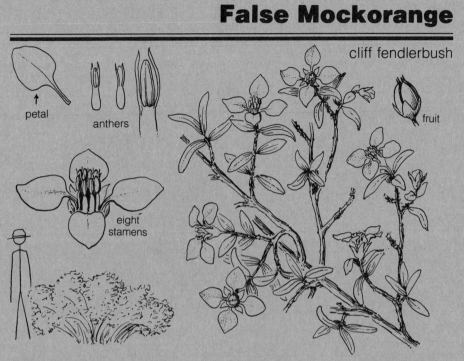

cliff fendlerbush

petal

anthers

eight stamens

fruit

Fendlera rupicola Saxifrage family *(Saxifragaceae)*

Range: Our whole range; s. to Mex. Cliffs & canyon walls, 3,000' - 7,000'.

Closely related to mockorange (opposite). It is similar in appearance and its blossoms are so much like it, that the two are hard to tell apart. They differ in that false mockorange has 8 stamens in contrast to 15 to 60 of the mockorange. It grows slightly taller — to about 6 feet. The 4-petalled flowers are every bit as handsome and showy and are usually white, but sometimes tinged with pink. Its narrow, acornlike fruits are gray green and about ½ inch long.

Paired, long and narrow leaves are about an inch long, slender, but thickish and often rolled under along the margins. New bark is lustrous reddish tan, becoming grayish and shreddy as it grows older, helping to distinguish this species from mockorange.

As with other species in the saxifrage family, false mockorange shows a preference for crevices in rocky canyon walls and ledges. As a consequence, it was given the Latin name *rupicola,* meaning rock-dweller.

Gooseberries, currants and hydrangeas as well as mockoranges belong to the saxifrage family. Saxifrage means "rock-breaker," as many species take root in rock crevices (including this species), actually breaking open the rocks when their roots enlarge while growing.

When other plants are scarce, it is browsed by mule deer, bighorn sheep and domestic goats, and to a lesser extent by cattle.

Golden Currant

flowering, fragrant or buffalo currant

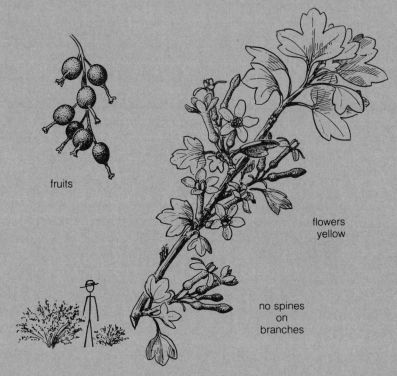

fruits

flowers
yellow

no spines
on
branches

Ribes aureum   Saxifrage family *(Saxifragaceae)*

Range: Our whole range; w. to CA; nw to WA; e. across U.S. & Can. to ND & Sask. Plains, hillsides & along creeks, 3,500' - 8,000'.

In spring, golden currant richly deserves its name — golden yellow clusters of long, trumpet-shaped, spicy-fragrant flowers adorn the bush in abundance. Gourmets eat the raw flowers, finding them delightfully tasteful.

The fruits of this currant are relatively large (marble size), and may be any color ranging from yellow through red, but more often black to purple black when fully ripe. They are sweet and edible as they come from the bush, but can be made into unusual jams and jellies, delicious pies and a unique ice cream.

The spineless bush itself ranges from about 2 to 6 feet tall with mostly 3-lobed, glossy green leaves.

Various Indian tribes often used the berries, either fresh or dried. The dried fruits, when mixed with dried, powdered buffalo meat, made pemmican, from which usage the name "buffalo currant" was derived. Fat was added to form cakes for future use or emergency rations.

Frémont Barberry

Frémont holly-grape, bérbero, agracejo [small grape], palo amarillo [yellow wood]

flowers

Berberis fremontii

Barberry family *(Berberidaceae)*

Range: Our whole range; w. to CA; n. to Can.; s. to Mex. Infrequent, well-drained soils, 4,000' - 7,000'.

This barberry was named for General John Charles Frémont (1813-1890) who led two expeditions to California (1843-44 & 1845-47), thus becoming the first botanical collector in the Sierra Nevada. He was not only a soldier and explorer, but also the first United States Senator from California and ran, unsuccessfully, for president of the United States. From 1878 to 1882 he was governor of Arizona Territory.

"Holly-grape" indicates that its leaves are much like spiny holly leaves and its fruits like grapes, though in miniature. A holly-grape is the floral emblem of the State of Oregon.

Other barberries are usually small shrubs with slender stems not exceeding 3 feet in height, but Frémont's usually grows from 5 to 10 feet tall, sometimes reaching almost treelike proportions to 15 feet! Its small yellow flowers are in bunches of 3 to 9 and develop into small (less than ½ inch) dark blue, miniature, grapelike berries. They make excellent jellies and jams.

The leaves consist of 3 to 7 leaflets, each about an inch long and ½ inch wide. Their wavy margins consist of about 3 large teeth on each side, with each tooth ending in a very sharp prickle.

Berberis extracts are used to some extent as bitter tonics. Yellow dyes are made from its roots and stems.

Many species of barberry are used for foundation plantings, not only for their shiny green, hollylike leaves, but also for the touch of color they add to the winter landscape. The leaves turn various shades of red and purple in the fall and remain on the plants throughout the winter.

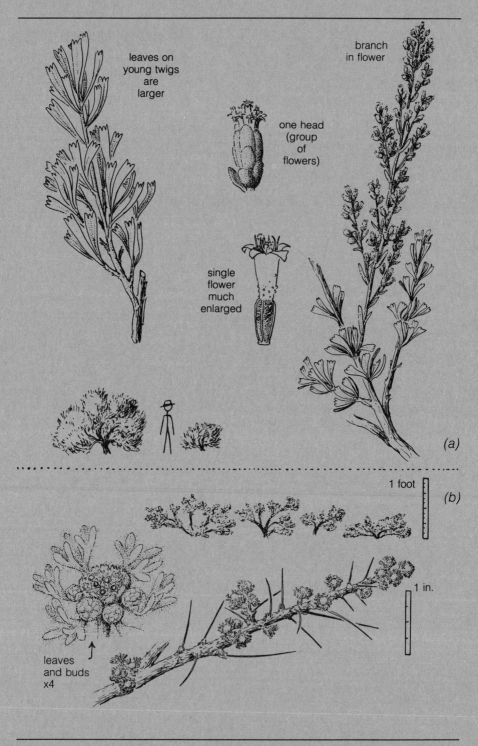

leaves on young twigs are larger

branch in flower

one head (group of flowers)

single flower much enlarged

(a)

1 foot

(b)

1 in.

leaves and buds x4

Big Sagebrush *(a)* basin sagebrush, common sagebrush, black "sage," blue "sage," "wormwood," chamiso hediondo [stinking chamiso], estafiata(e)

Artemisia tridentata Sunflower family *(Compositae)*

Range: Our whole range; w. to CA; n. to Can.; e. to NB; s. to Mex. Dry plains, mesas & rocky places, 4,500' - 10,000'.

Big sagebrush is one of the most widely known shrubs of the Southwest, covering vast acreage, sometimes to the exclusion of almost all other plants.

So abundant is it in Nevada that it has become their floral emblem, and the state is nicknamed the Sagebrush State.

It usually grows to between 2 and 7 feet tall, with a trunk to 3 inches in diameter. On favorable, moist sites it has been known to grow to tree size.

As this is one of the plants which causes hay fever, it is not universally loved, although its pungent odor is known to many, especially after a rain.

There is no mistaking the 3-parted leaves which are silvery hairy and wedge shaped. The young silvery stems turn dull gray and shreddy with age.

Big sagebrush is eaten by the sage grouse and small animals, and is browsed by deer, pronghorn, cattle and sheep. It played an important part in the lives of pioneers, as well: as medicine, food and fuel. Its wood smoke is so pungent that the Indians used to steep themselves in it to help neutralize the effects of an encounter with a skunk.

Sagebrush and sage are often confused, sagebrush being shortened to sage at the drop of a Stetson. Sages used for seasoning are not obtained from these plants, but from members of the mint family. "Land of the Purple Sage" (from Zane Gray's *Riders of the Purple Sage*), is an often-heard expression and possibly refers to this species of sagebrush.

Bud Sagebrush *(b)* spiny sagebrush, budbrush, bud "sage"

Artemisia spinescens Sunflower family *(Compositae)*

Range: AZ, NM, CO, UT; w. to CA; n. to MT & OR. Dry slopes & mesas, often in alkaline flats, 4,000' - 8,000'.

This sagebrush is like no other — its flower stems become one-inch-long woody spines when it ceases to bloom and the flowers have fallen. Like all sagebrushes, it is pungently aromatic when crushed or bruised. Growing only about a foot in height, it is scarcely noticed until it blooms in early spring, at which time it becomes a mass of small yellowish green flowers. Its leaves are grayish hairy and finely divided into from 5 to 7, 3-parted lobes, less than ½ inch long. The young stems of this plant are hairy white and the older stems have brown, fibrous bark.

It is considered by sheepmen to be a very valuable browse plant for their sheep, and it recovers quickly from overbrowsing.

It receives its name from the fact that the clusters of leaves and flowers resemble buds.

California Brickellia

brickellbush, pachaba

Brickellia californica
Sunflower family *(Compositae)*

Range: Our whole range; w. to CA; s. to Mex. Rocky washes & dry, gravelly slopes, 3,000' - 7,500'.

This is one of two woody-stemmed brickellias growing within our range — opposite is the other, the tasselflower. This species is a medium-size, rounded bush from about 1 to 3 feet in height and very aromatic. The flowers are small and clustered. They are yellowish white to creamy green, sometimes tinged with purple. They bloom from June to November. Short, fine hairs cover the rather thick leaves which are stubby and triangular shaped and rough to the touch. This plant is usually found growing among rocks in dry streambeds or on rocky hillsides.

The Gambel's quail (named for Dr. Gambel of Gambel oak repute), that jaunty little bird of river valleys and bottomlands, eats its seeds.

Pachaba is the Hopi word for this plant and they are reported to rub it on the head for headache. It is quite aromatic when crushed.

Tasselflower

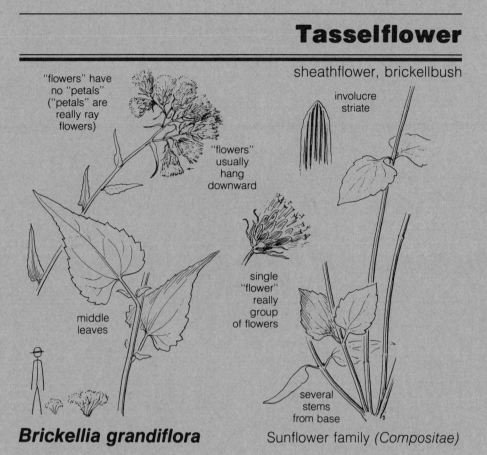

"flowers" have no "petals" ("petals" are really ray flowers)

"flowers" usually hang downward

involucre striate

single "flower" really group of flowers

middle leaves

several stems from base

Brickellia grandiflora

Sunflower family *(Compositae)*

Range: Our whole range; w. to CA; n. to WA & MT; e. to AR & MO; s. to Mex. Rich soils, 5,000' - 10,000'.

This, and the closely related California brickellia (opposite) are very similar looking and relatively hard to tell apart. These are some of the differences to look for: flowers in tasselflower usually hang downward (usually erect is California brickellia); flower clusters in this species are on the ends of the stems, whereas in the other species, the clusters are scattered along the branchlets; leaves are longer: more arrowhead shaped than stubby triangular — thin versus thick; and this brickellia grows in richer soils along streams, rather than in dry, rocky places.

Both brickellias grow to about 1 to 3 feet tall, the California species tending to slightly more woodiness.

The tasselflower receives its name from the drooping flowerheads, which look even more like tassels after they have gone to seed. The down of the seeds is quite white, making the bush more attractive at this stage than when in flower.

Its only known use is by the Navajos who mix it with other plants to make a liniment for the Female Shooting Life Chant.

Threadleaf Groundsel

felty groundsel, creek senecio, Douglas ragwort, old man, squawweed, yerba cana [gray-hair plant]

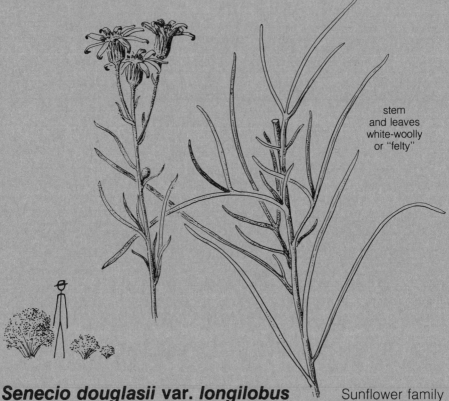

stem
and leaves
white-woolly
or "felty"

Senecio douglasii var. *longilobus*

Sunflower family
(Compositae)

Range: Our whole range; s. to Mex. Sandy washes & dry, gravelly streambeds, 2,500' - 7,500'.

Of these 2 groundsels, only this one's stems, leaves and bracts are covered with permanent woollike matted hairs. One to 3 inch long leaves with several narrow leaf divisions differentiate this species from broom groundsel (opposite) which has entire leaves with 1 or 2 short lobes at their bases. This species is an erect yellow-flowered bush which grows from about 18 inches to 3 or 4 feet tall (unusually to 6 feet): broom groundsel grows usually not over 24 inches.

The Navajo used the fuzzy tops as whisks to brush the spines from cactus fruit. They also boiled the whole plant and drank the brew to insure "good voice" for singing certain ceremonial songs.

Broom Groundsel

broom senecio, grass-leaved ragwort

Senecio spartioides
Sunflower family *(Compositae)*

Range: Our whole range; n. to WY & NB. Disturbed soils at roadsides & on rocky slopes, 5,000' - 9,000'.

A low, somewhat woody, bush with numerous sulfur yellow ray flowers, it grows only about 8 to 24 inches tall. It is common along roadsides, starting to bloom in July, and still blooming into September.

When the flower heads of this senecio (Latin: old man), as well as other senecios ripen, the silvery hairs attached to the seeds suggest the fluffy white hair of a senior citizen.

Worldwide, there have been reported over 2,000 species of senecios, some growing to tree size in South Africa. A species of senecio in Tibet is used in preparing *chong*, a spirituous and slightly acid liquor.

It is thought by some that perhaps the word "groundsel" comes from Old English "pus-absorber," as its chopped leaves were used in rural England as a poultice to reduce abscesses.

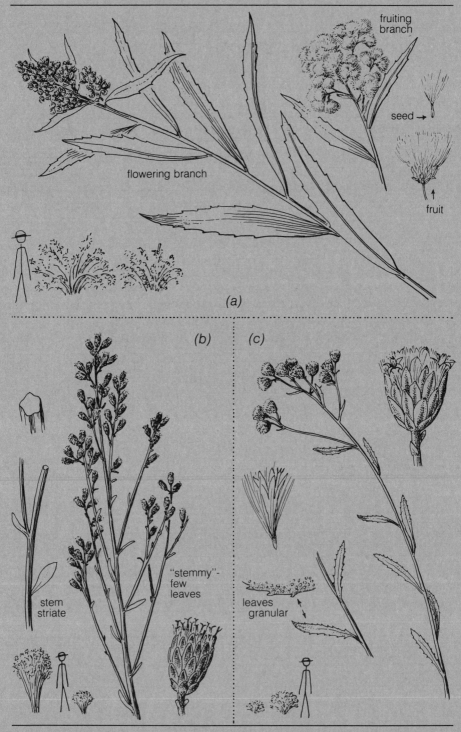

fruiting
branch

seed →

flowering branch

fruit

(a)

(b)

(c)

stem
striate

"stemmy"-
few
leaves

leaves
granular

76

Seep-willow (a)
sticky or broom baccharis; water-willow, water-wally, water-motie; batamote, yerba del pasmo

Baccharis glutinosa   Sunflower family *(Compositae)*

Range: AZ, NM, CO, w. TX; w. to CA; s. to Mex. & S. Am. Moist places, 2,000' - 5,500'.

Seep-willow derives its name from the fact that its leaves are willowlike and that it grows along seepage channels and watercourses. Its Spanish name implies that the plant (yerba or hierba) was used as a remedy for chills (pasmo). Another native name is yerba cana, meaning "gray-hair plant," in reference to its flowers after they have gone to seed. Some Indians used an infusion of the sticky leaves as an eyewash, while others chewed the stems to alleviate toothache.

The shrub is one of the most common ones seen along streambanks and irrigation ditches. It covers vast areas in the bottomlands of the Rio Grande. It likes to have its feet in the water and seems to prefer land that is occasionally inundated. Wherever it springs up it forms thickets and grows from 3 to 6 feet tall (sometimes to 12 feet). Its slender wandlike branches are smooth or finely grooved and about ½ inch in diameter. The branches end in numerous-headed flower clusters, which, when mature, produce fuzzy heads similar to old men's gray hair.

The leaves are bright, lustrous green, slightly sticky and 3 ribbed, particularly at their bases. They are also toothed and from 1 to 3½ inches long.

In Mexico, the stems are used for covering rafters of houses before the tiles are placed on them, for thatching temporary shelters and for makeshift brooms. The roots of a related species were used in ancient Greece to spice up wines.

Squaw Waterweed (b)
Baccharis sergiloides

Range: AZ & UT; w. to CA; s. to Mex. Moist places, 2,000' - 5,500'.

This baccharis differs from seep-willow (opposite) mainly because it is more broomlike and has fewer flowers. It blooms nearly throughout the year, but the dry heads quickly drop off when mature. In contrast, most of the leaves are absent at flowering time. It has sticky, 4 or 5 sided, finely grooved branches, and grows from 3 to 6 feet tall.

Arizona Baccharis (c)
Baccharis thesioides

Range: s. AZ, s. NM, w. TX; s. to Mex. Rocky, dry slopes, 4,000' - 8,000'.

This species has slender twigs which are, at first, green, but turn dark brown as they mature. In contrast to the other two baccharises, this one survives on dry, rocky slopes, growing to about 3 feet tall.

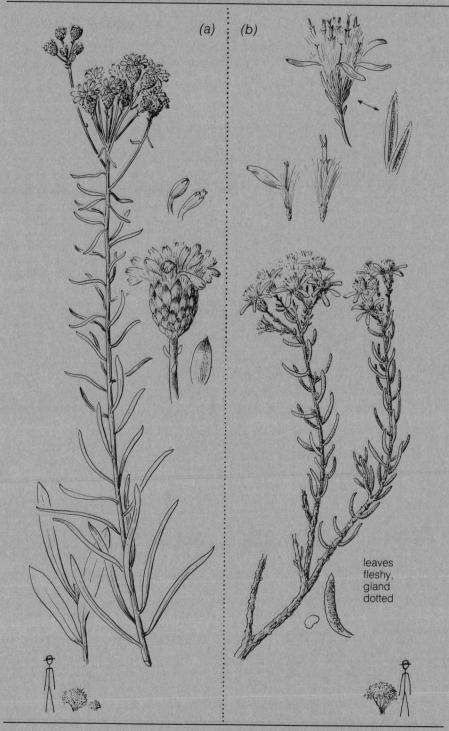

(a)   (b)

leaves
fleshy,
gland
dotted

(a) Jimmy-weed

jimmy goldenbush (-weed), rayless-goldenrod

Haplopappus pluriflorus   Sunflower family *(Compositae)*

Range: AZ, NM, CO, w. TX; s. to Mex. Dry plains & low hills, 1,000' - 6,000'.

Jimmy-weed differs from larch-leaf goldenweed in that its flowers have no rays along the margins of the flowerheads, but only tubular disk flowers in the central portion of the head; however, the flowerheads are very numerous and each head is many flowered. When the bushes are covered with their golden blooms from June to September, it truly is a handsome plant. It grows from 18 to 30 inches tall and readily invades overgrazed land and other disturbed areas such as roadsides.

Jimmy-weed is not usually eaten by livestock, generally being considered unpalatable because of its turpentinelike taste; but it is eaten as a last resort, such as during a drought when other plants are not available. It is quick to move into overgrazed range, and therefore more plentiful when cattle are hard up for forage.

When livestock, especially cattle, eat it in large quantities, it causes severe poisoning due to a toxicant that it contains. The ailment is called trembles in cattle, and can be transmitted to humans by eating dairy products or meat from the poisoned cattle. The human form is called milk sickness, an acute disease characterized by weakness, vomiting and constipation.

Jimmy is a corruption of jim-jams, a common name for delirium tremens, jitters or trembles.

(b) Larch-leaf Goldenweed

Haplopappus laricifolius   turpentine-bush

Range: AZ, NM, w. TX; s. to Mex. Dry, rocky hills & canyons, 3,000' - 6,000'.

When larch-leaf goldenweed is in full bloom from August to November, it is a solid mass of bright, golden yellow flowers. It is a toss-up as to whether this plant, jimmy-weed or broom snakeweed is the handsomest at flowering time. Its needle-shaped, larchlike leaves are somewhat fleshy, sticky with a resin and emit a turpentinelike odor when crushed.

This flat-topped, dense of leaf, shrub grows slightly taller than jimmy-weed — from about 18 to 40 inches.

This shrub is one of several Southwestern plants that was tested for its rubber content. Another was guayule, probably the best known, because it was raised commercially as a source of rubber. As larch-leaf goldenweed contained only about 2 per cent of rubber, it did not pay to raise it commercially.

The genus *Haplopappus* (sometimes spelled *Aplopappus*) contains very many species, but most are not shrubby. This species and jimmy-weed are the only two occurring nearly throughout our range which could be considered "woody."

Sticky-flowered Rabbitbrush

rabbitbush, goldenbush, rayless-goldenrod

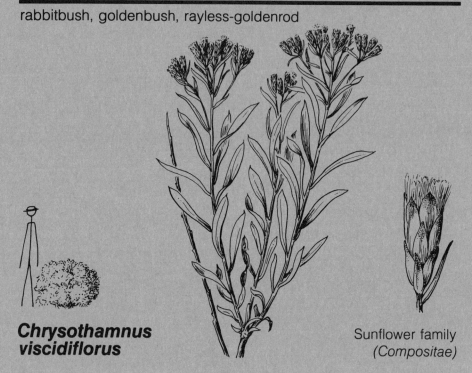

Chrysothamnus viscidiflorus

Sunflower family
(Compositae)

Range: Our whole range: w. to CA; n. to Can.; e. to NB. Dry mesas & slopes, 5,000' - 10,500'.

Rabbitbrushes blanket considerable areas of the Uplands with their golden flowerheads. They grow especially on poor, eroded or neglected lands.

This is a confusing species, with at least 7 subspecies being recognized, each of which intergrades with the others. Suffice to say, the *typical* sticky-flowered rabbitbrush is usually smaller than the golden rabbitbrush (opposite), growing, on the average, to only about 3 feet tall. Not only are the flowers sticky, but the whole bush itself is tacky to the touch. Its light green leaves are more or less twisted, linear and about ½ inch long.

Its name comes from the fact that rabbits use it for both food and as a favorite shelter. Its foliage and twigs are browsed by elk, pronghorn and deer. Small animals eat the flowers, and birds eat the seeds.

A tea is made from the leaves for "easing the stomach." Dried leaves and flowers are boiled and used as a tonic.

A yellow or light orange dye can be made by boiling the flowerheads with alum and lichens, but if the leaves and twigs are added, a soft olive green dye is produced. The Navajo used it as thatch for sweathouses, and the Indians of Utah and Nevada made a chewing gum from its roots.

Golden Rabbitbrush

rabbitbush, false "goldenrod", chamisa, chamiso blanco

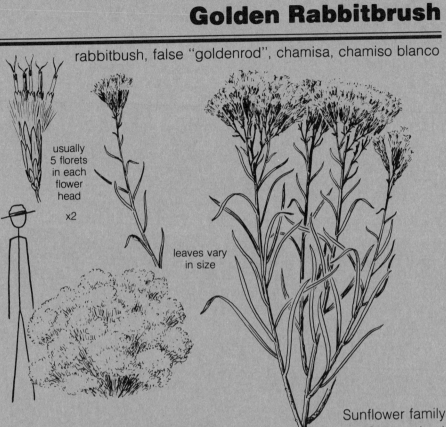

usually 5 florets in each flower head

x2

leaves vary in size

Chrysothamnus nauseosus

Sunflower family
(Compositae)

Range: Our whole range; w. to CA; n. to Can.; e. to ND & SD; s. to Mex. Dry slopes, mesas & roadsides, 2,000' - 8,000'.

In the fall of the year, golden rabbitbrush becomes very conspicuous, especially along roadsides and other disturbed areas, and well deserves the name "golden." Although each individual flower by itself is relatively small and insignificant, it grows in such dense masses of golden clusters that individuality is lost. Each flowerhead consists of up to a dozen tubular flowers, the whole no more than about ¼ inch broad. Numerous such heads are clustered loosely together into round-top groups.

The shrub itself grows about 2 to 5 feet tall (occasionally to 7 feet) and has woody, gray brown, shallow-fissured bark which sometimes becomes shreddy. The twigs are covered with feltlike matted hairs. The whole bush exudes a heavy aromatic scent.

The Hopi use the slender, flexible branches, stripped of bark, for basket making.

The foliage and seeds are eaten by browsing animals and rabbits.

Broom Snakeweed

brown-, broom-, yellow-, match-, sheep- or turpentine weed; match-brush; yerba de víbora, yerba de San Nicolás

Gutierrezia sarothrae   Sunflower family *(Compositae)*

Range: Our whole range; w. to CA; n. to Can.; e. to KS; s. to Mex. Disturbed soils, 2,000' - 8,000'.

This snakeweed is a subshrub from 8 to 24 inches high, so barely comes within the limits of a woody plant; however, it has a definite woody base, branching and rebranching until a rounded crown of fine twigs is produced. In the fall, small golden yellow flowers borne in numerous flat-topped clusters cover the entire plant, appearing like so many golden domes dotting the landscape from May to November. Its narrow leaves are 1 to 3 inches long and dotted with resinous glands.

The whole plant is somewhat resinous and has a heavy odor, hence the name "turpentine weed." "Broom" in its name is derived from the fact that Indians and Spanish-Americans use its stems for sweeping.

The names "snakeweed," yerba de víbora [rattlesnake weed] and sheep-weed come from the fact that when a sheep is bitten, the bite is treated by a poultice made of ground and boiled leaves of the plant; the swelling is said to go down immediately and the sheep cured.

Where broom snakeweed is abundant, it usually indicates that the land has been overgrazed, especially by sheep.

In New Mexico, the plant is boiled and the resulting liquid drunk for stomach disorders.

Spineless Horsebrush(-weed)

gray tetradymia, "black sage"

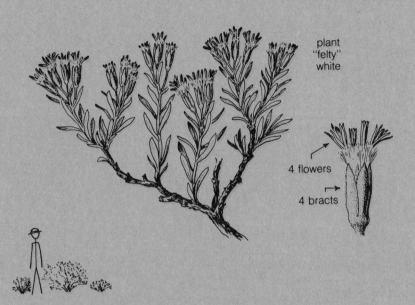

plant "felty" white

4 flowers

4 bracts

Tetradymia canescens Sunflower family *(Compositae)*

Range: AZ, NM, CO, UT; w. to CA; n. to Can. Dry, rocky or sandy soils, 4,500' - 9,000'.

Horsebrush is a freely branching, rounded, low shrub from 1 to 2 feet tall with numerous short, erect flowering branches from a woody base.

The flowerheads (p. 95) consist of 4 yellow disk flowers per head enclosed in 4 stiff, woolly scales. They are in clusters of up to 5 at the ends of the branches and bloom from June to September.

The twigs and numerous small, narrow leaves are densely silvery woolly. The older stems tend to lose their woolliness, becoming smooth and gray, with the bark eventually shredding into fibrous strips.

"Female ailments" were said to be allayed when the leaves and roots were used as a tonic by Hopi women.

When hungry sheep, especially after watering, eat large quantities of horsebrush leaves and stems, they may get bighead disease as a result of light sensitization. Fluid collects in the head, ears and neck and causes swelling that could bring death. Cattle seem not to be affected when they eat it.

Copperweed

ridgeplume, prickly oxytenia, blackroot

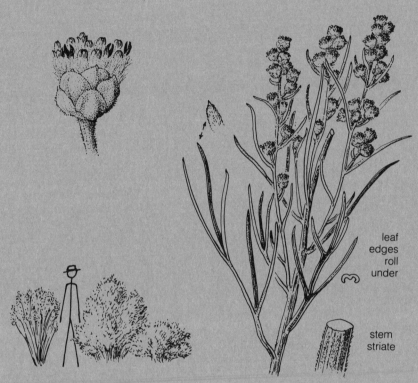

leaf
edges
roll
under

stem
striate

Oxytenia acerosa

Sunflower family *(Compositae)*

Range: AZ, NM, CO, UT; w. to CA. Dry plains & valleys, 3,500' - 6,500'.

A partly woody plant with rushlike stems characterize this 3 to 5 foot high shrub when it is leafless. When leafed out, it is covered with many slender, threadlike 3- to 5-parted leaflets whose edges are rolled under. The woody base is gray to brown, but the slender, fine-grooved stems that branch out from it are greenish to grayish and covered with stiff, rather short hairs lying flat against the stems.

It has been reported to be poisonous to sheep and cattle, especially where it grows in alkaline soils, but it is usually eaten only as a last resort. When ingested, poisoning is slow, consisting first of loss of appetite, then coma, and finally death with little struggle.

This plant has also been blamed for skin rash that seemingly develops in some people after brushing against it.

Western Hophornbeam

Knowlton hophornbeam, canyon ironwood

fruiting branch

female catkin

male catkins

Ostrya knowltonii

Birch family *(Betulaceae)*

Range: nw AZ, sc NM, sw UT, w. TX; s. to Mex. Isolated canyons, 5,000' - 7,000'.

This tree is easily recognized when it has gone to seed. The fruits consist of nutlets enclosed in flattened, pale green, papery, bladderlike husks which hang in groups and resemble clusters of hops. Its nearly oval, dark yellow green, birchlike leaves have saw-toothed edges and are about 1 to 2 inches long and are finely hairy beneath. They turn yellow in the fall just before dropping.

"Hornbeam" refers to the hard, horny nature of the wood. "Ironwood" also attests to the hardness of its wood which is close grained and heavy. Its wood is little used except locally for tool handles and similar small objects requiring hard wood.

Our hophornbeam can grow to tree size of 20 to 30 feet with a trunk diameter of about 15 inches; however, it is usually much smaller and shrublike. You'll be lucky to find this tree unless you really go looking for it, as it is in scattered locations: Grand Canyon National Park and Oak Creek Canyon in Arizona; the Guadalupe Mountains of southeast Arizona and western Texas; and in southeast Utah.

Western Soapberry

soaptree, jaboncillo [little soapy]

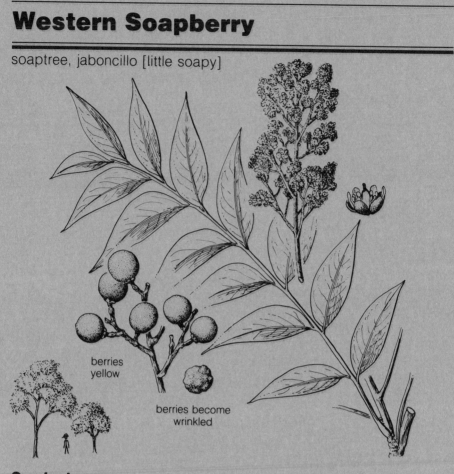

berries
yellow

berries become
wrinkled

Sapindus saponaria var. *drummondii*   Soapberry family
(*Sapindaceae*)

Range: AZ, NM, CO, w. TX; e. to MO, AR & LA; s. to Mex. & S. Am. Stream- &
canyonsides, 2,500' - 6,000'.

Early travelers did not discriminate between this tree and the nonnative
(and unrelated) Chinaberry with which they were familiar, writing "Wild China"
in their narratives when referring to this tree. It can grow to 40 or 50 feet in
height, but usually is not so tall, and sometimes it can be shrubby.

Small white flowers burst forth from the tree in early summer in many-
flowered pyramidal clusters. The yellow, translucent, waxen berries ripen later
and remain on the tree all winter, a good way to recognize the tree after its
leaves have dropped. The leaves consist of 9 to 17 ashlike leaflets.

The common name is derived from the fact that the seeds contain a
soaplike substance that forms a lather when placed in water and agitated.

Arizona Walnut

Arizona black walnut, nogal

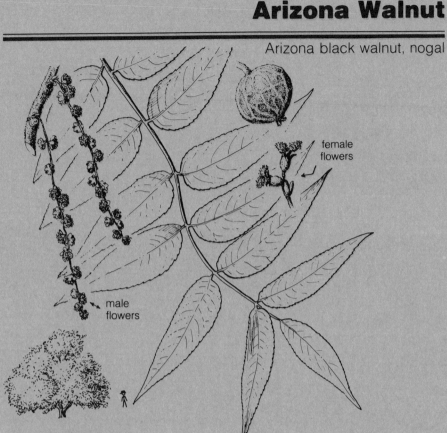

female
flowers

male
flowers

Juglans major

Walnut family *(Juglandaceae)*

Range: AZ, NM, w. TX; s. to Mex. Along watercourses, 2,000' - 7,000'.

Twelve species of walnuts grow throughout the world, 6 of which are found in the United States, so the tree should be familiar to nearly everyone. No one fails to recognize the commercial English (or Persian) walnut sold in our stores and markets.

All walnuts usually grow to tree size, ours to a maximum of 45 to 50 feet, with a trunk diameter of up to 4 feet, but usually smaller. Furrowed, scaly bark aids in identifying a walnut tree. The leaves are from 8 to 12 inches long and consist of from 9 to 13 (rarely 19) lance-shaped leaflets.

Long, drooping, separate male and female catkins appear on the same tree, the female producing nearly round fruits about 1 inch in diameter. These consist of an outer, almost smooth, husk and an inner deeply furrowed, hard-shelled nut which is similar to the black walnut fruit. If you can success-fully pry the small kernels from their convoluted repositories, you'll find that they are sweet tasting.

Desert Ceanothus

Gregg ceanothus, mountain balm, buckbrush, "wild lilac"

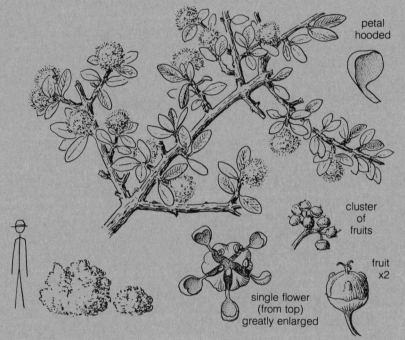

petal
hooded

cluster
of
fruits

fruit
x2

single flower
(from top)
greatly enlarged

Ceanothus greggii   Buckthorn family *(Rhamnaceae)*

Range: Our whole range; w. to CA; s. to Mex. Sandy soils, 2,000' - 7,000'.

It is unfortunate that there is no generally accepted common name for this genus, but "wild lilac" is often used, though it is not even remotely related to the lilac, just "looks like" it. Tongue-tied becomes he who tries to pronounce the plural of ceanothus.

This shrubby ceanothus seldom grows more than 5 feet tall and has crowded clusters of sweet-scented, white (occasionally bluish or pink) flowers in profusion. Its opposite, sometimes clustered, leaves are grayish green and concave above, gray beneath and quite thick and leathery. The olive green twigs become gray with age.

The leaves and blossoms of most ceanothuses make an acceptable "tea."

The principal wildlife use, besides cover, is browse for deer, elk and rabbits. Chipmunks and other small animals, as well as quail eat the small seeds.

Ceanothus is a large genus with 55 species in the world, 40 of which occur in the West. Three species are described in this booklet. (For the other two, see pine-oak belt).

Mockheather

James' frankenia

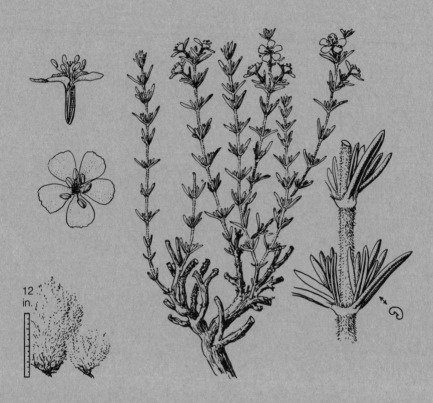

Frankenia jamesii   Frankenia family *(Frankeniaceae)*

Range: NM, CO, w. TX; w. to NV; s. to Mex. Alkaline or saline soils, 4,000' - 6,000'.

One of our dwarf bushes, belonging to its own distinctive family, but closely related to such diverse plants as camellia, ocotillo, passion flower, St. Johnswort, tamarisk, tea and violet.

It usually grows no taller than a foot or two, with small, frail-looking, white flowers. Its small leaves are awllike and the edges are rolled inward. They grow in crowded bundles, reminding some of the Old World heathers. It blooms from May to October around saline lakes and in alkaline soils.

The leaves of a species of mockheather which grows on the island of St. Helena (where Napoleon Bonaparte was exiled), were used as a substitute for tea.

Frémont Cottonwood

common or valley cottonwood; álamo, alamillo; (also called "poplar")

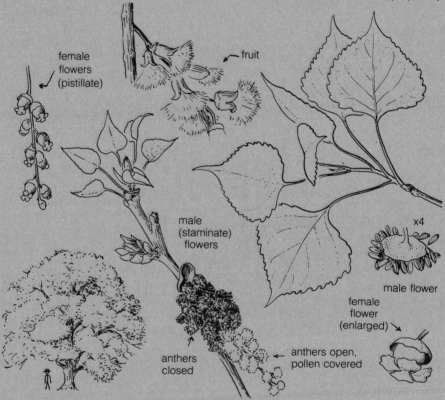

female flowers (pistillate)

fruit

male (staminate) flowers

x4

male flower

female flower (enlarged)

anthers closed

anthers open, pollen covered

Populus fremontii

Willow family (Salicaceae)

Range: Our whole range; w. to CA; e. to OK; s. to Mex. River valleys & riverbanks, 2,500' - 7,000'.

All cottonwoods bear the male and female flowers on separate trees. Mature seeds produced by the female catkins are covered with a white fuzzy cotton which gives the tree its name.

Frémont cottonwood differs from plains cottonwood (opposite) mainly by having slightly smaller and more coarsely toothed leaves. It reaches a maximum of 90 feet high and 5 feet in diameter, but usually it is about 50 to 60 feet tall and about 3 feet in diameter.

A variety, Rio Grande cottonwood (var. *wislizenii*) with coarser-toothed leaves grows in the Rio Grande valley from southern Colorado through New Mexico to west Texas and Old Mexico.

The trees turn a golden yellow in autumn just before the leaves fall.

Plains Cottonwood

Sargents cottonwood, plains poplar, whitewood, álamo

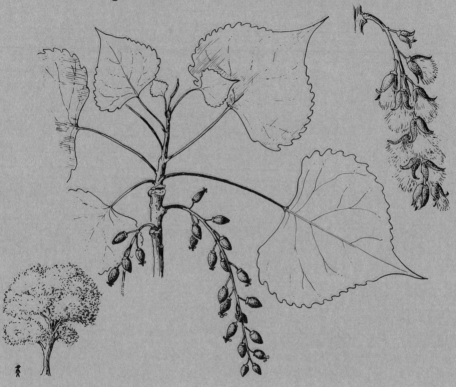

Populus sargentii

Willow family *(Salicaceae)*

Range: nw NM, e. CO, w. TX; n. to Can.; e. to OK & KS. Streambanks & moist places, 3,500' - 9,000'.

This cottonwood, under ideal conditions, will grow to 90 feet with a trunk diameter to 4 feet, but usually is more like 40 to 50 feet high and 2 to 3 feet through.

Cottonwoods (also called "poplars") were a welcome sight for early travelers in the Southwest as they grew not only where water was abundant (sometimes it was subsurface, but it was gladly dug for), but also its spreading canopy provided welcome shade from the hot summer sun for the travel weary.

The trees are commonly planted near homes and along streets for shade and along irrigation ditches as windbreaks. In order to avoid the fuzzy flying fluff of the female fruits, only cuttings from the male tree are planted.

From its wood the Navajo made many things — from prayersticks and tindersticks, through looms, to ceremonial duck effigies and dice.

Ephedras

Joint-fir family *(Ephedraceae)*

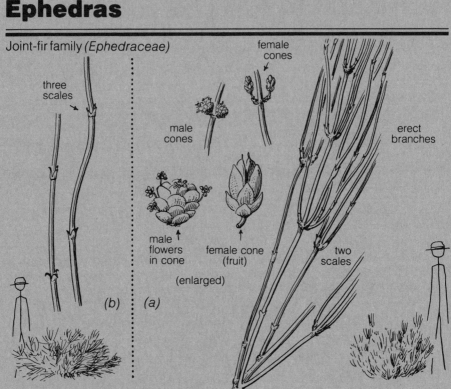

three scales

male cones

female cones

erect branches

male flowers in cone

female cone (fruit)

two scales

(enlarged)

(b)   (a)

Green Ephedra *(a)*   *Ephedra viridis*
joint-fir, Mormon tea, Brigham tea

Range: AZ, NM, CO, UT; w. to CA. Sandy areas, 3,000' - 7,500'.

This ephedra has bright green, finely furrowed, jointed stems, in upside-down broomlike clusters. The Navajo brewed the tops into a drink for use as a cough medicine. Other Indians roasted the seeds, ate them whole or ground them into a meal for various uses.

It is of more than passing interest to note that the ephedras are first cousins of the pines and junipers.

Some species found in Asia yield the drug ephedrine which is used in the treatment of colds and hay fever.

Torrey Ephedra *(b)*   *Ephedra torreyana*

joint-fir, Mormon tea, Brigham tea, Mexican tea, cañutillo [little tube], cañatilla [little reed], tepopote [little straw]

Range: Our whole range; w. to CA; s. to Mex. Sandy areas, 2,000' - 6,800'.

The jointed stems of this ephedra are olive green. From its dried stems, early pioneers brewed a hot drink, though the Navajo roasted the stems first, claiming that it improved the flavor.

The stems are sometimes grazed by cattle in the winter.

Redbud. In early spring the striking pinkish flowers appear.

Pinyon-Juniper Belt. Land of the pinyon and juniper — that vast expanse of the West betwixt the deserts below and the forests above.

a. Smooth Sumac. Its berries are used to make "lemonade."

b. Horsebrush. In early spring its golden heads dot the landscape.

c. Cliffrose. As delightful to look at in fruit as in flower.

d. Boxelder. Neither a "boxwood" nor an elder, but a maple.

Junipers (Often called "cedars."). Indians and early settlers used its wood, bark, twigs, berries, seeds and gum in various ways. Juniper "berries" are in reality modified cones, and because of their pungence, are used to flavor gin, a word derived from an Old French word for juniper: genèvre.

Rocky Mountain Juniper.   Common Juniper.   Utah Juniper.

Virgin's Bower. (right) Recognized in the fall because of its seed heads.

a.

b.

d.

e.

g.

h.

Pine-Oak Belt. The lowest of the true forest belts.

a. Ponderosa Pine. The commonest forest tree of the Southwest.

b. Fendler Rose. "Rose is a rose is a rose is a rose."

c. Mountain Gooseberry. Its tiny petals are hard to find among the petallike sepals.

d. Narrowleaf Cottonwood. Young trees are easily mistaken for willows.

e. Water Birch. Alderlike leaves and shiny red brown cherrylike bark identify this species.

f. Shrubby Cinquefoil. Its bright-golden-yellow roselike flowers bloom throughout the summer.

g. New-Mexican Locust. Its sweet-pea-like flowers immediately identify this as a locust.

h. Red-osier Dogwood. This dogwood is easily recognized by its bark: it is bright red.

i. Gambel Oak. Its acorns were a favorite with the Indians because they were less bitter tasting than those of other oaks.

99

Fir-Aspen Belt.

Aspen. In the fall, aspen groves turn brilliant gold.

There is no mistaking aspen bark, a favorite food of the beaver.

Mountain Lover. Truly named, as it is found almost exclusively at high mountain elevations.

Kinnikinnick, or Bearberry, as it is relished by bears.

Thimbleberry. Its red, squatty, thimble-shaped fruit is edible, but borderline in tastiness.

Fir-Aspen Grove. (right) In the midsections of the mountains, the white bark and light green leaves of the aspen contrast with the dark bark and dark green needles of the Douglas-fir.

Cones. All members of the Pine Family bear cones and are called conifers. You may be more familiar with woody pine cones, but perhaps not as familiar with those of spruce and fir. Above is an immature Engelmann spruce cone.

a. Subalpine Fir.
(Immature shown)

b. Douglas-Fir.

c. Bristlecone Pine.

d. Pinyon.
(Immature shown)

Lodgepole Pine.
e. (Male "flowers")
f. (Female cones)

a.

b.

c.

d.

e.

f.

Spruce-Fir Belt.   **Subalpine Fir.** The smallest of all the true firs .

Limber Pine. Its branches are so flexible they can be bent without breaking.

Treeline. Gnarled, stunted and grotesquely formed trees present weird sights in their struggle for survival at these frigid, windy heights.

Engelmann Spruce.

a. "Banner" tree.

b. Matted mass of "wind timber."

Bristlecone Pine.

c. Gnarled, open "grove."

d. Windswept "loner."

Pine-Oak Belt

(Approx. 6,500' - 8,000' elev.)

Just above the pinyon pines and the junipers and below the firs and aspens, the ponderosa pine (p. 98) and Gambel oak (p. 99) hold sway. They are the most representative plants of this belt — the lowest of the true forest zones. As compared with the areas immediately above and below, the pine-oak belt is intermediate in moisture supply, temperature and soil conditions; nevertheless the soil is still relatively dry and sandy, containing little or no humus. The average annual precipitation is between 20 and 25 inches.

From an economic standpoint, this belt, because of the presence of ponderosa pine, is the most important forested land of the Southwest. The forest may consist of widely scattered individuals, or the trees may grow in relatively open, parklike stands on rather dry hillsides and plateaus. In either case, the trees are tall, straight and evenly spaced, allowing sunlight to penetrate to the forest floor.

Because of the gradual transition between the lower pinyon-juniper belt and the higher fir-aspen belt, it is impossible to draw exact limits to mark the beginning and ending of the belt. Arbitrarily, therefore, the elevations between 6,500 and 8,000 feet have been chosen as the lower and upper boundaries of the pine-oak belt.

On the cool north slopes, the stands of ponderosa pine tend to be thicker, and the Douglas-fir intermingles with them; on the drier, lower slopes, pinyons intermix with the pines and oaks; and in the upper parts, aspen creeps downward to associate with the ponderosas.

Many shrubs characteristic of the pinyon-juniper belt also appear here where they usually reach their highest elevations: big sagebrush, rabbitbrush, snakeweed, boxelder and mountain-mahogany edge upward into the pines and oaks.

The following species straggle downhill into the upper edges of this belt: kinnikinnick, thimbleberry, raspberry, common juniper and honeysuckles.

Characteristic shrubs and trees of this belt, among others, are maples, serviceberry, bearberries, buckbrushes, hawthorns, roses, shrubby cinquefoil, snowberries and Rocky Mountain juniper. Along the streams, the narrowleaf and lanceleaf cottonwoods, thinleaf alder, water birch, chokecherry and an occasional blue spruce grow. Also found within this belt in the most southern portions of our range are the Arizona cypress as well as the Arizona, Apache and Chihuahua pines.

It is no wonder that this belt is sometimes called the Transition Zone, with so many species from three belts intermingling here.

There is a total of 50 plants listed in this section, but others creeping into this belt from down-mountain and up-mountain, more than double the number of species that may be found here.

Ponderosa Pine

western yellow pine, "black jack" pine, pino real [true pine], pinabete

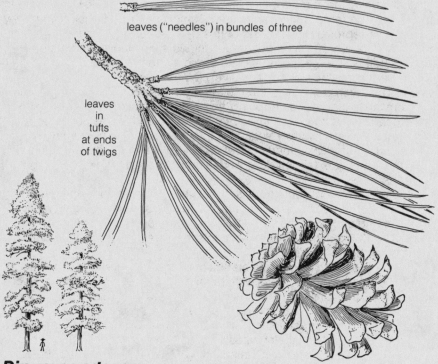

leaves ("needles") in bundles of three

leaves
in
tufts
at ends
of twigs

Pinus ponderosa

Pine family *(Pinaceae)*

Range: Our whole range; w. to CA, n. to Can.; e. to NB & the Daks; s. to Mex. Dry hillsides & mesas, 3,500' - 9,500'. Arizona var.: se AZ, sw NM; s. to Mex. 6,000' - 9,000'.

    This, the State tree of Montana, is easily identified by its 3 long needles (p. 98) and yellowish bark. It is a valuable forest tree and furnishes more lumber than any other American tree. It grows about 150 feet tall and 3 to 4 feet in diameter, larger trees living for 300 to 500 years. Young trees have a dark, almost black, bark which prompts the local name of "black jack."
    Children (and adults too!) have fun peeling scales from the tree trunks; the scales resembling all sorts of things: dolphins, rabbits, dogs, birds — and more!
    Indians ate the seeds either raw or made into a bread; squirrels and chipmunks as well as birds also enjoy eating them.
    The Arizona pine, with shorter cones and more slender needles in bundles of 5, is a variety of ponderosa pine (var. *arizonica*).

Gambel Oak

scrub, Rocky Mountain, Utah, white or blue oak

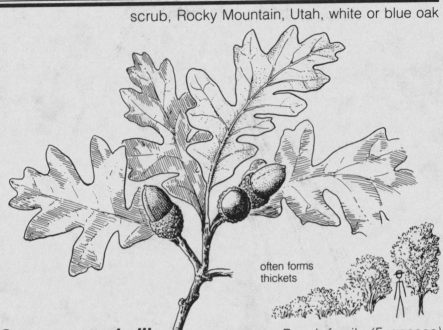

often forms
thickets

Quercus gambelii

Beech family *(Fagaceae)*

Range: Our whole range; w. to NV; n. to WY; e. to OK; s. to Mex. Dry hillsides & slopes, 4,000' - 8,500'.

Gambel oak is usually found in dense thickets within this belt, intermingling with ponderosa pine (opposite) on dry hillsides and slopes and occasionally along streams. Size is variable — from matted shrubs to low, shrubby trees. Its deciduous leaves are from 2 to 7 inches long and from 1½ to 3½ inches broad with 7 to 11 lobes. The indentations between the lobes reach more than one-half way to the midvein. The upper surfaces of the leaves are smooth, the under surfaces hairy. The male and female catkins appear on the same trees. Broadly oval acorns about 1 inch long are produced, held by a cup which about half encloses the acorn (p. 99).

The bark is grayish, rough and hard, becoming somewhat fissured with age. The wood is used in some areas for fenceposts and fuel.

Its acorns are preferred by the Indians because they are less bitter tasting than those of the "black" oaks. They were ground into a meal and leached in water until all bitterness (tannic acid) was gone. Mush, soup, bread and pancakes were then made, sometimes by combining the acorn meal with cornmeal.

An important browse plant for deer, it also provides shelter. If cattle feed on the leaves for too long a time they become constipated, emaciated and weak.

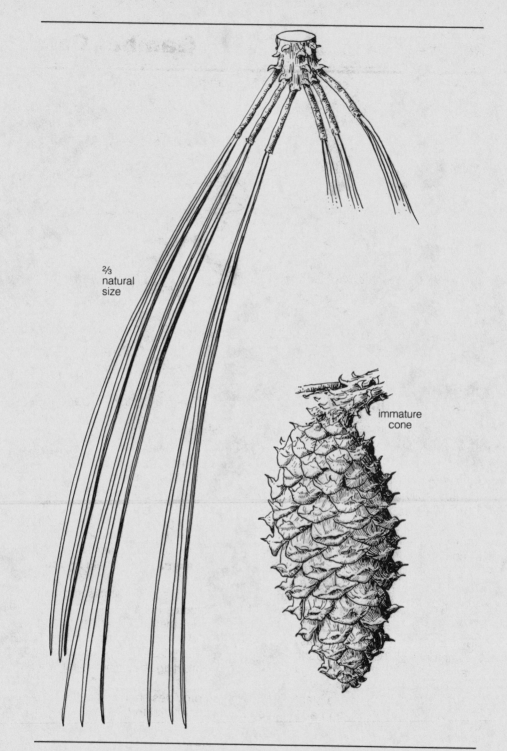

²/₃
natural
size

immature
cone

Apache Pine

Arizona longleaf pine, Engelmann pine

Pinus engelmannii

Pine family *(Pinaceae)*

Range: se AZ, sw NM; s. to Mex. Dry, sandy ground, 5,000' - 8,200'.

A pine of very limited distribution within our range, occurring only in extreme southwest New Mexico along the Continental Divide, in southeast Arizona and in the mountains of northern Mexico. It is very similar to ponderosa pine, especially in its old age (250 to 500 years), and is considered by some authorities to be only a form or variety of it. In youth (up to about 100 years), its needles are longer than the ponderosa's — to about 8 to 15 inches long (but mostly about 10 inches long), as compared to 4 to 8 inches long in the typical ponderosa. The needles are a clear, glistening green; ponderosa's are a darker green.

So remarkably do its long needles, in bundles of 3 (occasionally in bundles of 2 to 5), resemble the southern longleaf pine that many Southerners mistake it for their well-known pine. For comparative purposes, it grows to about 50 to 60 feet tall and about 1 to 2 feet in diameter, with a maximum of 75 feet and 3 feet through; whereas ponderosa pine grows to about 150 feet and 3 to 4 feet in diameter, with a maximum of 220 feet and 8 feet through.

The bark of the trunk is dark brown — slightly darker colored than ponderosa bark — but, as with ponderosa bark, it becomes yellow with age, and fissured.

Its oval cones are about 5 to 7 inches long and the cone scales are tipped with tiny prickles. The cones, usually in pairs, or in whorls of 3 to 5, are ocher colored. Ponderosa's are from 3 to 6 inches long and light reddish brown.

In contrast to the ponderosa pine, Apache pine is not sufficiently abundant to be of commercial value.

Apache pine was so named because its range roughly coincided with the old Apache country.

The inner bark of this, and other pines, was chewed or eaten by various tribes of Indians when in need of supplemental food. The Mescalero Apache remove the bark to obtain the resin that oozes from the inner bark for waterproofing their wicker water bottles.

Numerous birds and small animals eat its dark, coffee-colored seeds.

Rocky Mountain Juniper

western juniper, Rocky Mountain or western "red cedar," "scop" (horti-culture), cedro rojo [red "cedar"]

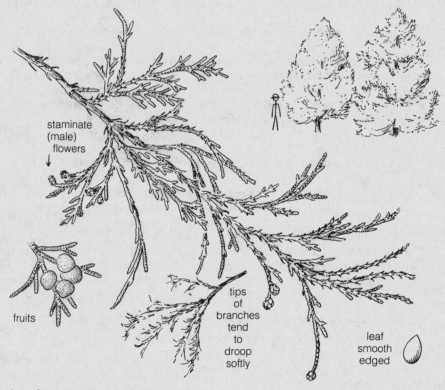

staminate (male) flowers ↓

fruits

tips of branches tend to droop softly

leaf smooth edged

Juniperus scopulorum — Cypress family *(Cupressaceae)*

Range: Our whole range; w. to NV; n. to Can.; e. to the Daks & OK. Low, rocky, mountain slopes and dry mesas, 5,000' - 9,000'.

This juniper is very similar to both Utah and one-seed junipers, but its needles are smaller, it grows more upright (p. 96), and has 2 (sometimes 3) seeds in its berries. Scalelike foliage and stringy bark are also characteristic of this species. It is the most widespread and treelike of the junipers, although it rarely exceeds 30 to 40 feet in height and 2 feet in diameter. Its bark is reddish to gray brown and scaly, becoming stringy and ridged on older limbs.

The pea-size, blue berries are juicy and edible (p. 96). The Indians ate the berries raw or cooked, or dried them for winter use. They are also an important source of food for birds and small animals.

Its wood is used for long-lasting fenceposts, fragrant fuel, lumber (especially "cedar" chests), pencils and novelties.

Arizona Cypress

cípres, "cedro"

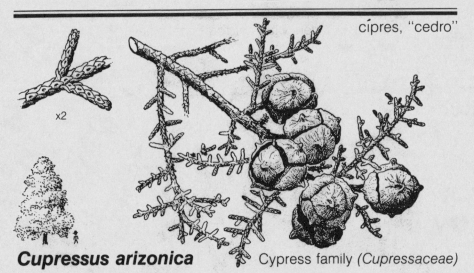

x2

Cupressus arizonica   Cypress family *(Cupressaceae)*

Range: se & c. AZ; sw NM; s. to Mex. In a few isolated canyons, moist or dry, rocky or gravelly slopes, 3,500' - 8,000'.

A handsome tree, growing mostly in Mexico, but extending northward into the United States where it is found in a few isolated canyons: Sabino, Stronghold and Bonita Canyons in southeast Arizona, and in the canyons of the Continental Divide in extreme southwest New Mexico.

When fully grown, it is usually no more than 40 feet tall and 2 feet in diameter. Its scalelike, gray green leaves are similar to those of junipers, but in contrast to them, they have dark, red brown globular cones about 1 inch in diameter with woody scales. The cones open at maturity, spilling their myriad (90 to 100) tiny seeds, and remain on the tree for years. (Juniper cones are fleshy, remain closed, and contain only from 1 to 4 seeds.)

Cypress bark is reddish brown and scaly when young, to fissured and fibrous when old, often checkered like alligator juniper bark.

In the Southwest it is planted extensively as an ornamental, a smooth-barked form being preferred. It is also commercially grown and sold for Christmas trees.

Arizona cypress is a close relative of the famous Monterey cypress and the ornamental Italian cypress. Old World cypresses are famous for their longevity, some, it is said, live more than 2,000 years. The original doors (now bronze) of St. Peter's church in Rome were made of Mediterranean cypress and stood for over 1,100 years (A. D. 335-1506).

Cypress was sacred to Pluto, and since early times was used as a symbol of mourning, and more recently, of immortality. Its branches, at funerals, were placed at the door and around the funeral pyre of the deceased, especially if he were a person of social importance.

Water Birch

Rocky Mountain, canyon, black or red birch; abedul

twigs rough with
large glands

fruit ("cone")
solitary

Betula occidentalis

Birch family *(Betulaceae)*

Range: AZ, NM, CO, UT; w. to CA; n. to Can. Streambanks & moist locations, 5,000' - 9,000'.

Water birch is often associated with its near relative, thinleaf alder. Both plants are easily recognized by their miniature pine-cone-like fruits. Those of water birch are solitary and cylindrical and disintegrate when mature; those of alder are in clusters, nearly round and remain whole. Another way of telling these two apart is by their barks: that of water birch is a shiny red brown and cherrylike (p. 98), while that of thinleaf alder is grayish in tone. Water birch bark is broken by horizontal markings that enlarge as the stems grow.

In our range, water birch may reach a height of 10 to 25 feet with a trunk diameter of up to 10 inches. More usually it grows in 6 to 8 foot clumps and is more shrublike with a trunk averaging less than 8 inches in diameter. It commonly forms impenetrable thickets, especially along streambanks.

Its 1 to 2 inch leaves are thin and dull green, nearly oval and doubly toothed. They turn a golden yellow in the fall.

In pioneer days, slender birch twigs (more technically called birch rods) were used to "birch" unruly school children. A reminder of olden times endures in the expression "spare the rod and spoil the child." Its long, straight stems have often furnished emergency fishing rods for school children playing hooky, necessitating the later use of a "rod" at home or in school.

river, mountain or black alder; aliso, baraña

fruit ("cones") clustered

Alnus tenuifolia

Birch family *(Betulaceae)*

Range: ne AZ, n. NM, CO, UT; w. to CA; n. to AK; s. to Mex. Along mountain streams & lakeshores & in wet meadows, 4,500' - 10,000'.

Thinleaf alder is abundant along mountain streams or in moist meadows, in nearly impenetrable shrubby stands with several stems less than 4 inches in diameter emerging from the same rootstalk. Under favorable conditions it may grow taller to become a small many-stemmed tree to 30 feet in height, some of the stems attaining diameters of about 6 inches.

The oval to oblong leaves are larger than those of water birch, averaging from 2 to 4 inches long and 1½ to 2½ inches wide. They are doubly toothed, the main teeth having smaller teeth on them.

The woody scales of the female catkins persist and look like miniature pine cones.

Alder bark is rich in tannin and very puckery if chewed. Because of its tannic acid content, the bark is used in Mexico for tanning, giving skins a red color. It is used for dyeing blankets as well.

Alder leaves used with alfalfa leaves, fennel and endive are reported to make an excellent spring tonic.

Beavers, deer and rabbits eat the bark in spite of its puckery taste (to us, anyway). Many species of birds feed on the seeds.

California Buckthorn

coffee-, pigeon- or "bear-berry"; yerba del oso [bear's (medicinal) herb]

underside of
leaves soft-
hairy

petals
tiny

Rhamnus californica   Buckthorn family *(Rhamnaceae)*

Range: AZ, NM; w. to CA; n. to WA; s. to Mex. Rocky, sheltered canyons, hills & mountainslopes, 4,000' - 7,000'.

A shrub commonly from 5 to 9 feet high with gray branches and purplish twigs. Its 1½ to 4 inch long, elliptical to oblong leaves are glossy green and finely toothed and remain on the plant all year.

Small, inconspicuous, greenish flowers appear in May and June. The berries turn from green to red to purple black as they mature and have been used as a coffee substitute, hence one of the common names.

At least 7 species of birds have been recorded as eating the fruit. Black bear and mule deer are also known to eat the berries. It is a relatively important plant for the honey industry, as bees often use California buckthorn as a source of nectar.

This species, as well as birchleaf buckthorn (opposite), are first cousins of cascara buckthorn whose dried bark yields cascara [Sp.: cáscara] sagrada [holy bark] used as a mild laxative. It was "holy" because the Franciscan missionaries of early California first learned, from the Indians, that it had medicinal properties.

Even though this species is called "buckthorn" it is not thorny.

Birchleaf Buckthorn

coffeeberry, ramno

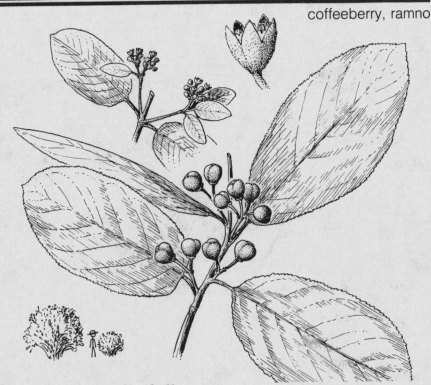

Rhamnus betulaefolia
Buckthorn family *(Rhamnaceae)*

Range: Our whole range (CO?); w. to NV; s. to Mex. Usually along streams, 4,000' - 7,000'.

This buckthorn tends to be shrubby and grows up to 15 feet tall and up to 4 inches in diameter. As with California buckthorn (opposite), this species also has tiny, greenish flowers with minute petals. Fleshy, shiny black to dark purple fruits ripen in the fall.

Its minutely toothed, deciduous leaves are thinnish, deeply veined and birchlike, the upper surfaces bright green, smooth and shiny, and the lower surfaces paler or even sometimes downy. The trunk bark is smooth and gray to dark gray, while the young, greenish to reddish twigs are covered with short, soft hairs.

The buckthorns were first used as medicine by the Indians, then the settlers. Though people find the fruits bitter, they are relished by many species of wildlife. Its twigs and foliage or also browsed.

This species is a nonthorny buckthorn. All species of buckthorn seem to contain cascarin, a relatively mild laxative.

Mogollon Ceanothus

deerbrush, California or white "lilac," mountain "birch," white tea-tree, soapbush

fruit

Ceanothus integerrimus   Buckthorn family *(Rhamnaceae)*

Range: AZ, NM; w. to CA; nw to WA. Sunny, dry sites, 2,000' - 7,000'.

Called "deerbrush" because, like most ceanothuses, it is a valuable deer browse. In California this browse plant is rated one of the most valuable for livestock.

A rather handsome, much-branched shrub, it is usually no more than 8 feet tall. It has large, bright green leaves and narrow, pyramidal, loosely branched "lilaclike" flower clusters of small whitish blooms which are sometimes pinkish or bluish. The fruit is a dry capsule with a slight crest.

The bark of the root of this shrub is used as a remedy for numerous ailments, including colds, liver disorder and malaria. The bark was used by Southwest Indians as a tonic and for making a soapy lather when stirred in water, hence the name "soapbush." California Indians used the long, flexible shoots for basketry.

The leaves of an eastern species, called New Jersey tea, were used as a tea substitute during the American Revolution. A western species, Oregon tea, has also been used similarly.

Several species of birds, not the least of which is the quail, are reported to eat the small, hard seeds. Rabbits and porcupines nibble the bark. It is common knowledge that good honey comes from bees using its flowers as a nectar source.

It receives its common name because it grows in abundance on the Mogollon [pronounced muggy-OWN] Plateau in east-central Arizona and west-central New Mexico.

Fendler Ceanothus

Fendler buckbrush, deerbrush

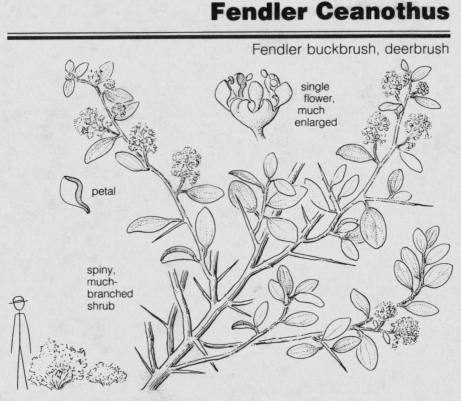

single flower, much enlarged

petal

spiny, much-branched shrub

Ceanothus fendleri

Buckthorn family *(Rhamnaceae)*

Range: Our whole range; n. to WY; e. to SD; s. to Mex. Pine forests, 5,000' - 10,000'.

This species of ceanothus is the only one of our three that is a spiny shrub. It is a low bush, seldom growing over 3 feet high, often forming thickets. It blooms mostly in June and July, but has been known to bloom as early as April and as late as October, depending on the weather and altitude. The blooms come all at one time, covering the entire plant with numerous clusters of small, white flowers. The thick, grayish green leaves are dense woolly hairy beneath. Twigs and young stems are gray green, turning a reddish brown as they mature. The spines are straight, slender and sharp and up to one inch long.

The dried leaves of this shrub were occasionally used as a tea substitute. Its small fruits were used for food by Indians from the pueblos of Laguna and Acoma, while the Navajo made a remedy for "alarm and nervousness" from it and green gentian. The mixture was used both externally and internally.

Fendler ceanothus is a favorite browse plant for deer in spite of its spines. Porcupines eat it and it is nibbled by jackrabbits. Domestic livestock occasionally munch on it.

Sulfurflower

sulphur eriogonum, "umbrella plant"

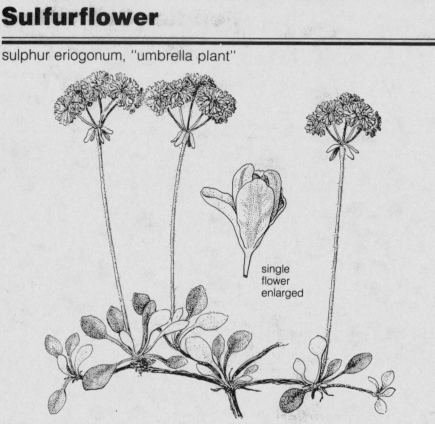

single flower enlarged

Eriogonum umbellatum   Buckwheat family *(Polygonaceae)*

Range: AZ, CO, UT; w. to CA; n. to Can. Dry, sunny locations in well-drained soils, 4,000' - 10,000'.

Bright yellow flowers in dense, flattish, umbrellalike clusters give the sulfurflower its names. As the flowers mature, they turn red, then brown and remain on the plant throughout the winter.

The plant's base is woody, and from this spring the annual herbaceous, 4 to 12 inch high leafless flowering stalks. Clusters of green leaves which are woolly white beneath surround the stem bases. The stems, at first, are woolly white, but with age, lose some of the woolliness. A few leaflike bracts occur where the main stem branches to form the ribs of the umbrellalike flowerheads.

The buckwheat family is most famous for its seeds which not only are used for buckwheat cakes, but also for horse and poultry feed. Other members of the family are rhubarb, knotweed and dock.

Several species of birds and small animals use eriogonum seeds, flowerheads and leaves as food, and mule deer and mountain sheep browse the plants.

Creeping Barberry

creeping holly-grape, "Oregon grape," yerba de la sangre, sangre de Cristo

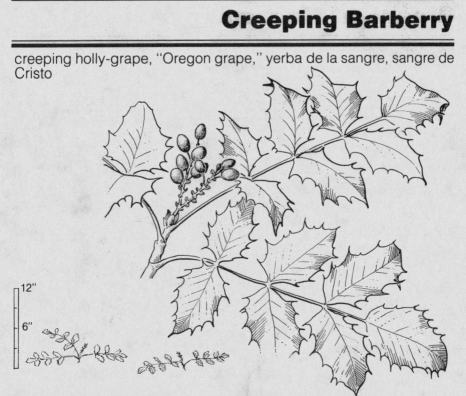

12"

6"

Berberis repens

Barberry family *(Berberidaceae)*

Range: Our whole range; w. to CA; n. to Can; s. to Mex. Thickly wooded, well-drained slopes, 5,500' - 10,000'.

This barberry, unlike its relative of the pinyon-juniper belt, seldom grows over a foot high. It, too, has hollylike leaves, but with more waves in their margins, hence more spiny-tipped teeth. Although the shiny green leaves of the creeping barberry are evergreen, they change to various shades of red or purple in the fall. The creeping stems root wherever they touch the ground.

Small, yellow, fragrant blossoms, borne in clusters, are followed by blue black, pea-size berries which can be eaten from the bush, but their flavor is supposedly improved after they are dried. They make good jellies, especially when the juice is mixed half and half with apple juice. Sometimes they are crushed in water, a minimum of sugar added, to produce a lemonadelike drink.

An infusion of twigs and leaves was used by the Navajo as a treatment for rheumatism; in fact, berberine, an alkaloid extracted from barberry bark is a medicinally useful tonic. The Spanish-American names indicate that a tea of roots or leaves was drunk to cleanse the blood and to cure anemia.

In early times a spray of barberry was considered a potent charm against witches.

123

Greenleaf Manzanita

green manzanita

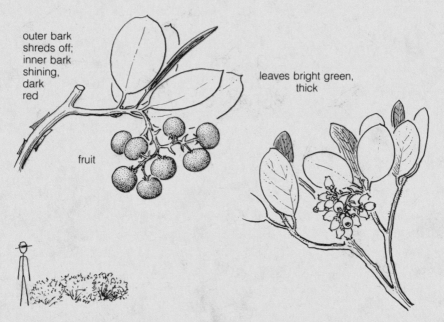

outer bark shreds off; inner bark shining, dark red

leaves bright green, thick

fruit

Arctostaphylos patula

Heather family *(Ericaceae)*

Range: AZ, CO, UT; w. to CA; nw to OR. Open ground & forest openings in well-drained, acid soils, 6,000' - 9,000'.

Greenleaf is easily distinguished from pointleaf manzanita (opposite) in that its leaves are thicker, nearly oval and bright green. The thick leaves of this species stand vertically with their edges toward the sun, an arrangement that retards evaporation.

Grotesquely twisted, mahogany red stems help to identify this species. They glisten in the sun as though they were freshly varnished.

Waxy, urn-shaped flowers in dense, numerous-flowered, drooping groupings identify it as belonging to the heather family. The blossoms are pinkish white with their rims tinged with darker pink.

"Manzanitas" [little apples], shaped like flattened marbles are yellowish brown to creamy white and follow the flowers.

The Indians used the fruits either raw, cooked or dried. It is reported that the unripe fruits can be made into delicious jellies. Leaves and fruits are said to have a diuretic effect when eaten.

All manzanitas provide food and cover for many species of birds and animals. Deer, and occasionally goats, browse the twigs and leaves.

Pointleaf Manzanita

manzanilla, pingüica

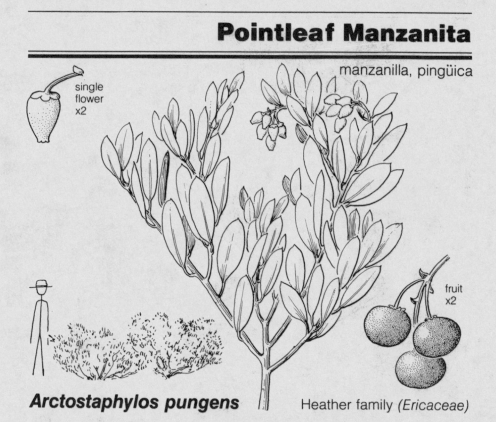

single flower x2

fruit x2

Arctostaphylos pungens　　　Heather family *(Ericaceae)*

Range: AZ, NM, UT, w. TX; w. to CA; s. to Mex. Dry, sunny slopes & rocky mesas, 3,000' - 8,000'.

    This manzanita grows in large bushy clumps 3 to 6 feet tall. As its branches sometimes take root where they touch the ground, it tends to form dense, quite extensive, thickets. Its trunk is dark mahogany color, but the branchlets are covered with dense hairs, giving them a grayish appearance in contrast to the red branchlets of greenleaf manzanita (opposite). The long-oval, sharp-pointed leaves are pale bluish green due to the soft, fine hairs covering their rather leathery surfaces. The berries are chestnut brown to terra cotta in color and look like shiny, flattened marbles.

    Of nearly 50 species of manzanita, 36 are native to the United States. The dozen or so others are largely Mexican, and the fruits of this species are occasionally seen in the native markets. The Mexicans make a delicious jelly from its fruits.

    "Herbaleros" [herbalists] prescribe: "50 berries and 50 leaves for each cup of tea or 15 grams of leaves (or 30 berries) per liter of water," "to be taken 3 times a day." As a diuretic it is "magnífico." It also "cures" any number of other afflictions, running the gamut from albuminaria and bronchitis to venereal diseases.

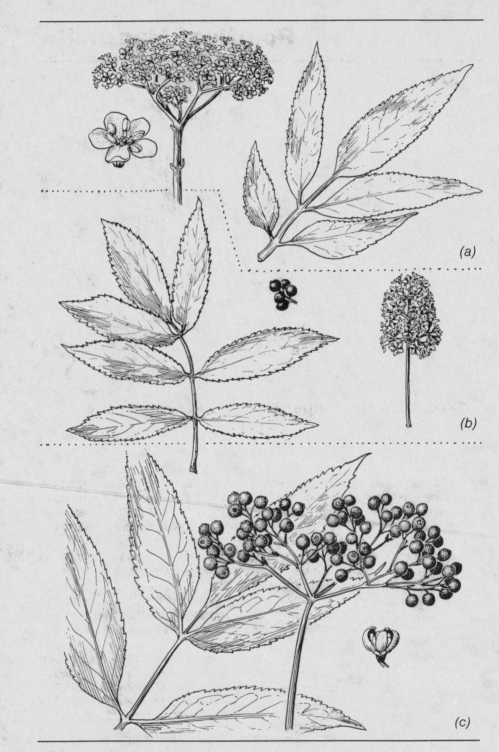

(a)

(b)

(c)

Elder, Elderberry, Saúco

Sambucus species
Honeysuckle family *(Caprifoliaceae)*

"Elder" has its origin in the Anglo-Saxon word *ellen,* meaning "fire-kindler." Its dry, pithy stems *do* make good kindling.

The fruits of all species are more or less edible, and are widely used for making jellies, pies, tarts, syrups and wine. (Eating redberried elder has caused severe intestinal upset in some people.) The blossoms can be used to make "elder blow" wine by adding raisins and yeast. Early colonists used elderberry juice as a cure for rheumatism.

Blueberry Elder *(a)* blue elderberry *Sambucus coerulea*

Range: Our whole range; w. to CA; n. to Can.; s. to Mex. Moist soils, canyon bottoms, along streams & on hillsides, 5,500' - 8,000'.

More treelike than the other two elders: to 20 feet tall and 8 inches in diameter, but is usually closer to 8 feet tall and 4 inches in diameter.

Flat-topped to umbrella-shaped clusters of delicate white flowers terminate the branch ends. The resulting berries are dark blue and covered with a whitish, powdery coating (bloom) and are in rather dense clusters.

The leaves are composed of from 5 to 9 smooth-surfaced leaflets, green above, but paler below.

A favorite of the Indians who ate the berries fresh, cooked or dried.

The fruits which are barely palatable to us are an important source of food for many species of birds. Robins become so eager for the fruits that they sometimes consume them before they are fully ripe.

Blackbead Elder *(b)* *Sambucus melanocarpa*
black elderberry, mountain elder

Range: AZ, NM, CO; w. to CA; n. to Can. Along streams & on mountainsides, 5,000' - 9,500'.

Aptly named, as its berries resemble clusters of shiny black beads. Unlike the other two elders, its berries have no powdery coating.

The flower clusters differ from the other two by being pyramidal in shape.

The shrub rarely grows taller than about 9 feet; more usually from about 4 to 6 feet.

Birds, deer and other wildlife eat the berries and foliage.

New Mexican Blueberry Elder *(c)* *Sambucus neomexicana*
New Mexican blue elderberry, "capulí or capulín" [wild "chokecherry"]

Range: AZ, NM, CO. Moist, protected places & along streams, 5,000' - 9,500'.

New Mexican blueberry elder is considered by some botanists as a variety of blueberry elder, differing only by having narrower leaves and blue black berries with a white bloom.

It grows from 6 to 12 feet tall and has creamy white flowers in dense flat-topped clusters.

Several browsers feed on the foliage and birds, squirrels and other rodents eat the fruits.

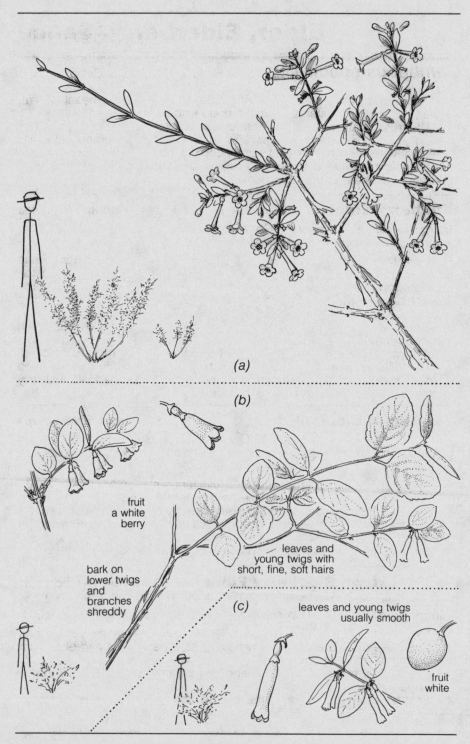

(a)

(b)

fruit
a white
berry

bark on
lower twigs
and
branches
shreddy

leaves and
young twigs with
short, fine, soft hairs

(c)

leaves and young twigs
usually smooth

fruit
white

Snowberries

Symphoricarpos species Honeysuckle family *(Caprifoliaceae)*

These plants are easily recognized in the fall by their most distinctive feature: showy snowy-white berries which give them their common name.

Many species are cultivated as garden shrubs because of these distinctive berries.

They are important shrubs for wildlife: providing not only food, but also nesting sites for birds and protective cover for both birds and animals.

Longflower Snowberry *(a)*

Symphoricarpos longiflorus

Range: Our whole range; w. to CA; n. to OR. Rocky slopes, canyons & valleys, 4,000' - 8,000'.

This snowberry is a 2 to 4 foot high shrub with its young stems brown (sometimes sparsely hairy) and its older stems whitish to gray and fibrous and shreddy.

Its pale green leaves are elliptic and the flowers are pink, trumpet shaped and very fragrant. The white, waxy-looking berries are pea size and eaten by many species of birds and small animals.

Roundleaf Snowberry *(b)*

Symphoricarpos rotundifolius

Range: AZ, NM, CO, UT; w. to CA; n. to WY. Dry, rocky slopes, canyons & valleys, 4,000' - 10,000'.

This snowberry is a low shrub, usually about 2 feet tall with slender, brown, fuzzy-hairy twigs which turn gray and become shreddy with age.

The leaves are rounded and thickish, their upper surfaces dull grayish green and soft hairy and their lower surfaces paler and with longer, soft hairs. The flowers are pink to rose colored and have shorter tubes than mountain snowberry. The white, globular berries persist through most of the winter.

Cattle, sheep and goats browse its twigs and foliage.

Mountain Snowberry *(c)* wolfberry, "buckbrush"

Symphoricarpos oreophilus

Range: Our whole range; w. to CA; n. to WY; s. to Mex. Wooded mountain slopes, valleys & riverbanks, 5,500' - 10,000'.

This snowberry is a well-shaped shrub from 2 to 5 (or sometimes 7) feet tall with smooth twigs, which, with age, turn brown and become shreddy.

Its leaves are thin, smooth and oval, light gray green above and paler below. The berries are a snowy, porcelainlike color and highly noticeable but not very tasty.

Indians made medicine from the roots.

Arizona Honeysuckle

madreselva

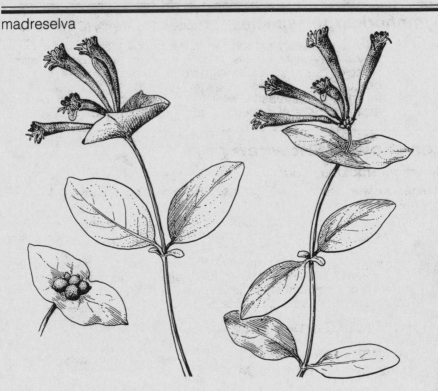

Lonicera arizonica   Honeysuckle family *(Caprifoliaceae)*

Range: AZ, NM, UT, w. TX. Open coniferous forests, 6,000' - 9,000'.

Because the flowers are rich in nectar ("honey"), they are "sucked" by hummingbirds, thus giving rise to the name "honeysuckle."

Showy, red, trumpetlike flowers with orange throats, growing in clusters help identify this clambering, woody vine. Spherical red berries are produced and are eaten by several species of birds and small animals. They *are* edible, and some people *do* eat the berries; however, it is reported by some that they act as a purgative.

The trailing, woody stems vary from gray to brown, their barks becoming stringy and shreddy with age.

There are about 150 species of honeysuckles in the world, 24 of which are native to the United States. They are most abundant in Asia, and the Japanese species is "naturalized" in the United States and has become a pest in some places.

Flowers of Old World species are sometimes used for making perfumes, and a syrup of the fruits has been used for treating asthma.

Virginia Creeper

thicket creeper, American "ivy," "woodbine"

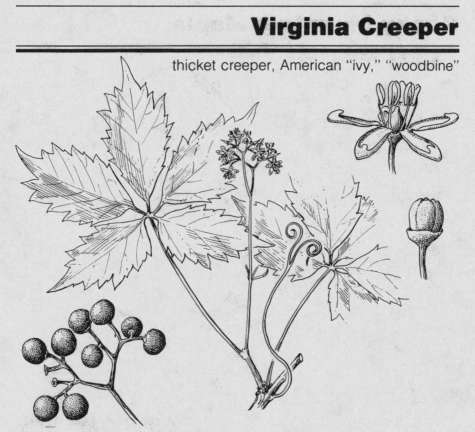

Parthenocissus vitacea

Grape family *(Vitaceae)*

Range: Our whole range; n. to WY; ne to OH & MI; s. to Mex. Streambanks, roadsides & fences, 3,000' - 7,000'.

Like its relative, wild grape, Virginia creeper seems to prefer moist, sunny clearings along fences, roadsides and streambanks, rambling casually over bushes, trees and fences indiscriminately.

It differs from eastern Virginia creeper by not having aerial roots nor sucking disks on its tendrils, differences minor enough that some botanists consider this a variety of its eastern cousin.

Its woody stems, when young, are reddish to brownish, but become gray brown with age and somewhat fissured.

Small, greenish flowers appear in June and July in open flat-topped clusters. Grapelike bunches of small, bluish black fruits follow in August and September and remain on the vines into winter, unless the birds and small animals get there first.

The thin, five-fingered leaves are dark green and shiny above, but lighter and thinly downy beneath. They turn scarlet in the fall.

Rocky Mountain Maple

smooth maple, dwarf maple

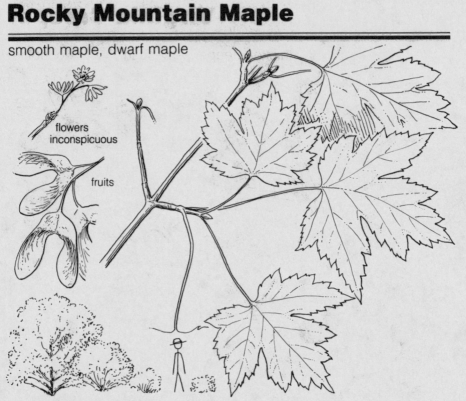

flowers
inconspicuous

fruits

Acer glabrum

Maple family (Aceraceae)

Range: AZ, NM, CO, UT; w. to CA; n. to AK; ne to SD. Moist, deep soils of canyons & mountainsides, 5,000' - 10,500'.

This maple is usually a many-stemmed shrub from 6 to 12 feet tall, but often it grows to small-tree size from 20 to 30 feet with a trunk diameter of 6 to 12 inches, especially in the deeper woods under a canopy of larger trees. It is handsome and well formed with smooth, light gray to gray green bark.

Its numerous leaves are typically maplelike: 3 (or 5) lobed, but with coarsely toothed edges. The leaf stems are red and the leaves are shiny green above and paler green below.

The fruits are called "keys" or "samaras," which are nothing more than a pair of seeds with broad, parchmentlike wings joined together. The keys are attractive, ranging in color from pale green to rose. When the keys mature in the fall they slowly twist and turn their way to Mother Earth to fulfill their destiny.

In the fall, Rocky Mountain maple is not as colorful as some of the other forest shrubs and trees, but the leaves do turn a pale yellow to reddish orange before they drop.

Squirrels and chipmunks eat the seeds, and moose, elk and deer browse the foliage. Birds eat the seeds, buds and flowers.

Bigtooth Maple

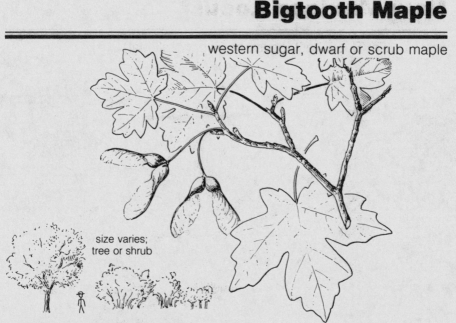

western sugar, dwarf or scrub maple

size varies;
tree or shrub

Acer grandidentatum

Maple family *(Aceraceae)*

Range: Our whole range; w. to CA; n. to AK; e. to NB & OK; s. to Mex. Canyon- & hillsides, in rich, moist soils, 4,500' - 8,000'.

Bigtooth maple is sometimes considered to be a variety of the eastern sugar maple. The Indians used it for making sugar and for seasoning foods. They also used the pounded bark to make "bread."

It can grow to small-tree size of about 35 feet, on the average, with a trunk diameter of about 9 inches (or it can be a large, usually several-stemmed shrub 8 to 12 feet tall). As with Rocky Mountain maple (opposite), the leaves are broken into 3, sometimes 5, lobes. These are broad and blunt and not finely toothed as in Rocky Mountain maple. They are larger, dark green and lustrous above, paler and hairy beneath.

The bark, in contrast to that of the Rocky Mountain maple, is light brown (sometimes gray) with shallow furrows and flat-topped ridges.

The leaves, just before falling, turn a beautiful red, orange or yellow, livening up the autumn landscape.

Deer as well as livestock browse the twigs and foliage.

The keys, as in all maples, break from the tree at maturity, the twin wings serving to rotate them, thus increasing their horizontal flight as they are wafted away by the wind.

Maples are often planted as shade trees, especially along city streets. The hard, light-colored, close-grained wood is used primarily for flooring and furniture. Markings resembling eyes of birds gave rise to the name "bird's-eye maple." Its wood makes excellent fuel.

New-Mexican Locust

pink, rose or Southwest locust; hojalito [small leaf]

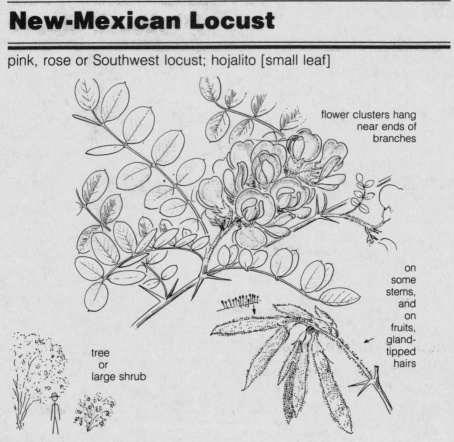

flower clusters hang
near ends of
branches

on
some
stems,
and
on
fruits,
gland-
tipped
hairs

tree
or
large shrub

Robinia neomexicana

Pea family *(Leguminosae)*

Range: Our whole range; w. to NV; s. to Mex. Valley bottoms, canyonsides and streambanks, 4,000' - 8,500'.

   Showy, pale pink to rose colored, sweet-pea-like flowers in large, dense, drooping clusters (p. 98) appear in early summer and immediately identify this as a locust tree. If it is not in bloom, look closely at the leaves and their stems. The leaves are divided into 9 to 21 finely hairy leaflets on a stout fuzzy brown stem. At the stem base are two paired, leaflike points which turn into sharp, stout, brownish red thorns from ½ to 1 inch long. A prick from a thorn feels like a bee sting.
   The fruits are hairy brown, pealike pods.
   The shape and size of this locust varies from shrubby (6 to 10' feet) to treelike, but small and crooked (to 25 feet).
   New Mexico Indians ate the flowers raw.
   Quail and squirrels eat the seeds; mule deer, goats and sheep browse it; and cattle are especially fond of the blooms.

narrowleaf, three-leaved or western hoptree; wafer-ash, shrubby trefoil, telea, cola de zorillo [skunk tail]

Ptelea angustifolia   Rue family *(Rutaceae)*

Range: Our whole range; w. to CA; s. to Mex. Shady, rocky slopes at woods' edges, 3,500' - 9,000'.

A tall shrub or small tree up to 20 feet high. Small, pale yellow to greenish white, fragrant flowers burst forth about mid-May in dense clusters. They are followed by drooping bundles of winged, somewhat hoplike fruits. After the leaves drop in the fall, the fruit clusters stand out against the bare branches — a positive means of recognition.

Another sure way of identifying the hoptree during the rest of the year is by its 3-parted, lustrous, dark green leaves. They emit, according to some, a very disagreeable odor, but to others they "smell something like hops."

The fruits are very bitter and have been used as substitutes for hops in brewing, as they would impart, like hops, a bitter flavor to malt liquors.

It gets its name, then, either because it looks like hops, smells like hops or is used like hops, or perhaps because of all three!

The roots have been employed as a remedy for indigestion and as a mild tonic. At one time they were used as a substitute for quinine in allaying malaria and fevers. Because of this, the bark was once known as ague bark. As with barberry, it has been found to contain an alkaloid, berberine, a useful, though bitter, tonic.

Some people develop dermatitis after contact with this plant.

Rue, grapefruit, lemon and orange belong to this family.

Utah Serviceberry

shadberry, -bush or -blow; Juneberry

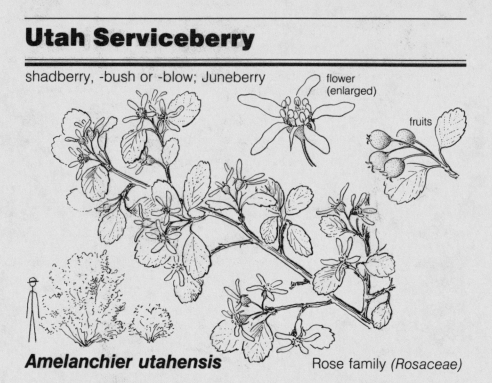

flower (enlarged)

fruits

Amelanchier utahensis   Rose family *(Rosaceae)*

Range: AZ, NM, CO, UT; w. to CA; n. to Can. Moist, rocky hillsides & streambanks, 4,000' - 10,000'.

Serviceberry is very conspicuous in early spring when dense clusters of peculiarly fragrant white blossoms cover the bush before the leaves appear. It can be a tall shrub or a small tree from 6 to 15 feet high. Its leaves are alderlike and have teeth only above the middle.

In the fall, its small, bluish purple, blueberrylike fruits ripen. They are slightly sweet and frequently used for jams, jellies or pies, and occasionally for winemaking.

In the early days the berries were a favorite food of many Indian tribes who ate them fresh or dried them for later use. They also ground the dried fruits and mixed them with jerked venison or buffalo meat and melted fat to make pemmican, an important concentrated provision for long journeys or for winter food. Explorers, hunters and soldiers adapted the formula by using raisins, beef, suet and sugar. As Army "K rations" its nutritional quality, and especially its palatability were often debated.

The slender, straight, peeled branches were used by the White Mountain Apaches to form the uprights of their large carrying baskets.

The berries and foliage are a favorite food for over 60 species of wildlife.

In the West it is called serviceberry (or sarvisberry as oldtimers were wont to say); eastern species are called shadblow because its "blows" (blossoms) appear in the spring when shad are running upstream to spawn.

Antelopebrush

bitterbrush, buckbrush, "greasewood"

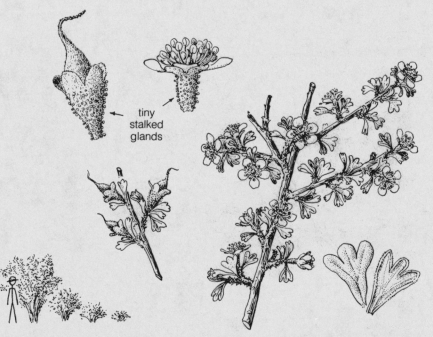

tiny
stalked
glands

Purshia tridentata

Rose family *(Rosaceae)*

Range: AZ, NM, CO, UT; w. to CA; n. to Can. Dry, usually rocky hillsides & slopes, 3,500' - 9,000'.

Antelopebrush is a low, silvery to gray, much-branched, spreading shrub, reaching up to about 2 to 10 feet in height. From April to August it is covered with many tiny, fragrant, pale yellow blossoms which are usually solitary and very attractive. Its leaves are about 1½ inches long and about ⅛ to ¼ inch wide. They are wedge shaped, have thrice-notched tips somewhat resembling stubby big sagebrush leaves. The leaf margins are turned under and the leaves are thinly hairy and greenish above and densely matted and lighter below.

The small, tapered capsules are yellowish tan tinged with orange red. They are densely hairy, tailed and contain black seeds about the size of grains of wheat. They are intensely bitter if chewed, but apparently animals like them.

It is a favorite browse species of mule deer, and is browsed to a somewhat lesser extent by pronghorn and elk. To chipmunks, pocket gophers and ground squirrels, the seeds are an important source of food. Occasionally these small animals eat the foliage and rabbits nibble at it.

Fendler Rose

wild rose, rosal

thorns
slender,
nearly
straight

Rosa fendleri

Rose family *(Rosaceae)*

Range: Our whole range; n. to Can.; e. to KS; s. to Mex. Hillsides & roadsides, 3,500' - 10,000'.

All wild roses are easily recognized, since they are very similar everywhere. They all have showy, single, fragrant pink blossoms (p. 98), thorns and red "hips" for fruits. "Rose is a rose is a rose is a rose."

This species can grow to 8 feet tall. It has reddish stems and thin dark green leaves. Its thorns are slender and slightly curved in contrast to those of the Arizona rose (opposite) which are stout and strongly curved.

Rose hips can be eaten raw from the bush and are "good for you" as they contain large amounts of Vitamin A and are rich in Vitamin C. Jams, jellies and wine have been made from the hips.

Many kinds of birds and animals nibble the rose fruits.

Roses are so popular, worldwide, that they are depicted on the postage stamps of at least 50 different nations, including the United States.

Arizona Rose

wild rose

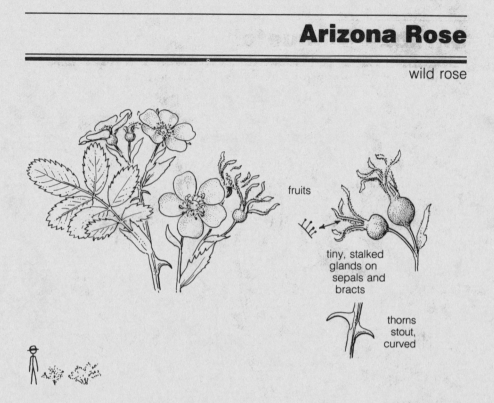

fruits

tiny, stalked glands on sepals and bracts

thorns stout, curved

Rosa arizonica

Rose family *(Rosaceae)*

Range: AZ, NM. Shady streamsides & forest edges, 4,000' - 9,000'.

This wild rose differs mainly from Fendler rose (opposite) by having smaller flowers and larger thorns. It grows smaller, to only about 1 to 3 feet high, and is much branched. Its stems are brown to whitish with flaking bark and bright green hairy leaves. Even botanists have trouble distinguishing rose species.

Roses have been the best known and loved flowers in many lands since prehistoric times. Dried rose bouquets were found in Egyptian tombs, and the Greek poet Sappho called the rose "queen of flowers" over 2500 years ago. They were sacred to Aphrodite, the Greek goddess of love and beauty, as well as a favorite flower of the Romans.

Rose petals and leaves were used medicinally in ancient times, and Roman naturalist Pliny (A.D. 23-79) listed 32 kinds of healing potions that could be made from them.

The rose is the floral emblem of England and of Georgia, Iowa, New York and North Dakota as well as the District of Columbia.

Old recipe for a sandwich spread: "Put rose petals and butter in covered jar for two days." Oleo can be substituted. Sounds "yummy."

Shrubby Cinquefoil

bush cinquefoil, five-finger, cincoenrama [five-leaf]

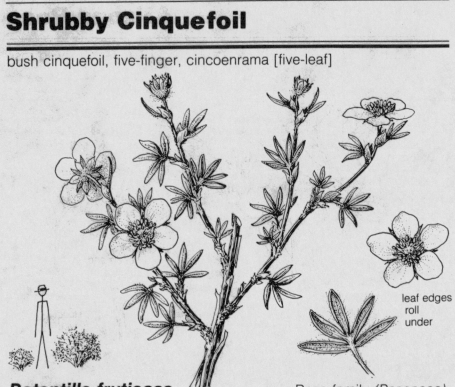

leaf edges
roll
under

Potentilla fruticosa   Rose family *(Rosaceae)*

Range: Our whole range; w. to CA; n. to AK; e. across U.S. & Can. to NJ, Lab & Gnld; s. to Mex. Also Gt. Brit., Eu. & Asia. Usually in moist places, but also in dry, shady places, 7,000' - 11,500'.

From Latin *quinque*, five, and *folium*, leaf comes the common name for this shrub. It has 5- (sometimes 3- to 7-) parted greenish leaflets covered with silvery gray, silky hairs. The leaves are somewhat whiter beneath and their edges curl under.

Showy bright-golden-yellow, 5-petalled, roselike blossoms (p. 99) in few-flowered clusters (Cover) appear in June and continue to bloom through the summer and into September. It grows normally to only about 3 feet high. Of the more than 300 species of cinquefoils throughout the world, this species is the only shrubby one. It is often seen as a cultivated plant.

Shreddy brown bark, together with the 5-parted leaves identify this cinquefoil when it is not in bloom. In winter, the brown, shreddy bark together with the brown fuzzy fruits help you in recognizing it.

This species was named by Linnaeus in 1753.

Since fevers in the olden days were blamed on wild spirits, a medicine that reduced fever was considered a potent agent against evil spirits. The name *Potentilla* for the genus is diminutive for "powerful" (potent) and arose from this belief.

Curlleaf Mountain-mahogany

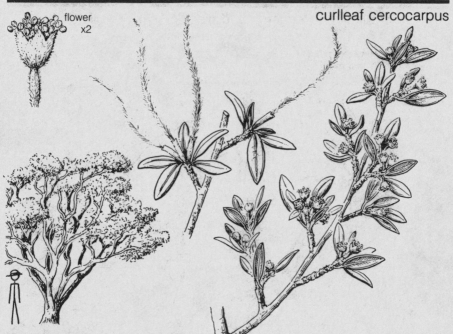

flower
x2

curlleaf cercocarpus

Cercocarpus ledifolius

Rose family *(Rosaceae)*

Range: n. & sc AZ, n. NM, w. CO, UT; w. to CA; n. to WA & MT; s. to Mex. Dry, gravelly slopes, 5,000' - 10,000'.

Immediately identifiable by its distinctive leaves: they are evergreen, aromatic, resinous and green above, and thick and leathery, with their edges slightly curled under (accounting for the common name). They are densely white hairy (sometimes rusty) beneath.

Small, yellowish flowers appear in profusion in early spring. In late spring and early fall the fruits appear, which are similar to all other mountain-mahoganies — about the size of a grain of wheat, to which is attached a long, plumy, corkscrewlike tail.

Normally, it is a rounded, reddish-brown-barked, scraggly shrub, but becomes a medium-size tree with 1 to several trunks that may reach 15 to 25 feet in height, with a trunk diameter of about a foot. On old stems the bark is broken up by shallow fissures.

Its wood is exceedingly heavy, hard and dense and is occasionally used for cabinet work (it takes a high polish), novelties for the tourist trade and roller skate wheels. It is valuable for fuel, but of greater value in the protection of watersheds from erosion.

Deer and elk use it as a browse plant, and thickets provide good cover for them as well as for small animals and birds.

Common Chokecherry

western or black chokecherry; wild black cherry, capulín

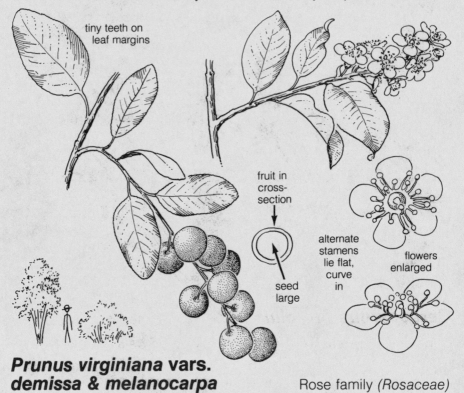

tiny teeth on leaf margins

fruit in cross-section

seed large

alternate stamens lie flat, curve in

flowers enlarged

Prunus virginiana vars. *demissa* & *melanocarpa*

Rose family *(Rosaceae)*

Range: AZ, NM, CO, UT; w. to CA; n. to Can.; e. to GA. Hillsides, canyons & streamsides, 4,500' - 9,000'.

This chokecherry, for our purposes, includes two western varieties of the common or eastern chokecherry. They can grow to tree size of about 15 feet, but more often they are found in loose thickets where they seldom exceed 9 to 10 feet.

Five-petalled white flowers are borne in cylindrical clusters 3 to 4 inches long.

The bitter, astringent taste of the fruits, especially if eaten before they are fully ripe, gave rise to the name "chokecherry." They are occasionally consumed by humans, but more often by bears who especially relish them.

The fruits, although nearly all pits, are very popular for making jelly, syrup and juice, not to mention wine. The bark has been used to make tea.

Indians of all tribes within its range highly esteemed the fruits. They ate them either fresh or dried them for later use.

Bitter Cherry

wild, quinine or mountain cherry; cerezo

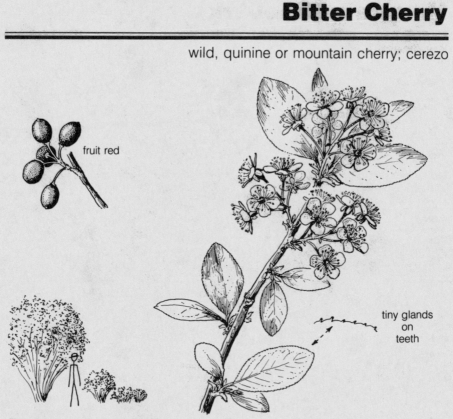

fruit red

tiny glands
on
teeth

Prunus emarginata

Rose family *(Rosaceae)*

Range: c. & se AZ, sw NM; w. to CA; n. to Can.; s. to Mex. Rich, sandy or gravelly soils along streams, 5,000' - 9,000'.

The bitter cherry is a rather small tree, growing only to about 15 feet tall and only a few inches in diameter, but mostly it tends to be shrubby, forming thickets.

It has a few dull white flowers in small groups, in contrast to numerous fragrant, white flowers in showy elongated clusters of the chokecherry (opposite). The fruit consists of a group of from 4 to 8 dark red (turning almost black) cherries, whereas chokecherry will have as many as 20 dark purple to black cherries in long clusters.

Bitter cherry receives its name because the fruits are intensely bitter and puckery. The twigs and foliage also have a bitter taste.

Its 1 to 3 inch leaves are small and oblong, finely toothed and a glossy, dark green. Its twigs are reddish brown when young, but turn dark red as the stems grow older. The bark is marked by small, orange, corky cells.

Indians ate the bitter fruits and made a tonic from the bark.

Mountain Ninebark

low ninebark

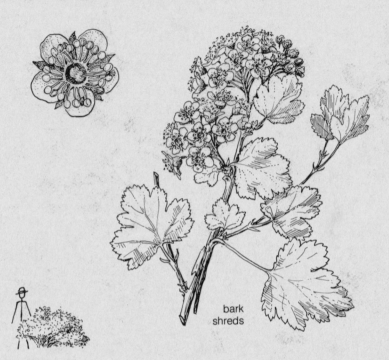

bark
shreds

Physocarpus monogynus   Rose family *(Rosaceae)*

Range: Our whole range; w. to NV; n. to WY & SD. Shady canyons & north slopes, 5,500' - 10,000'.

Ninebark receives its name from the fact that the old brownish bark is continually molting in thin, papery shreds, exposing each time a new layer of bark as if it had "nine lives."

Not a tall shrub — it barely reaches 4 feet in height — producing, in May, rather lovely white, or often rose-colored, flowers arranged in terminal umbrellalike heads. The petals arise from a cuplike structure. When the flowers go to seed they turn a reddish brown and remain on the shrub into winter. The inflated pods are white hairy.

Its leaves have 3 to 5 doubly toothed lobes and resemble large currant leaves. They are dull green on the upper surfaces, but lighter beneath.

The roots of ninebark were boiled by the Indians, and the resulting mass was placed, while still warm, on sores and lesions as a poultice to ease pain.

The Rocky Mountain goat feeds on its twigs in the winter when grasses and other weedy plants are buried deep under the snows.

Mountain Spray

rock-spiraea, creambush

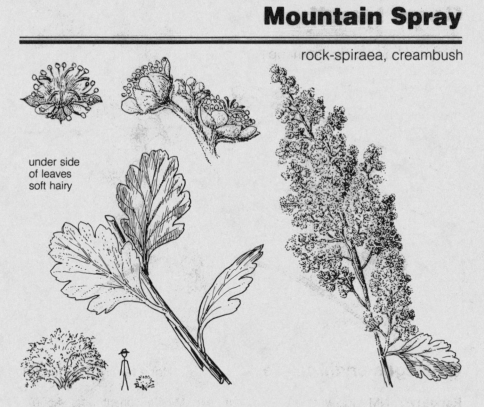

under side
of leaves
soft hairy

Holodiscus dumosus

Rose family *(Rosaceae)*

Range: Our whole range; w. to CA; n. to WY; s. to Mex. Rocky slopes & bases of cliffs, 5,500' - 10,000'.

    This is a beautiful and graceful shrub, growing usually from 3 to 6 feet tall. An abundance of small, but very showy, white to creamy white, or pinkish flowers are borne in pyramidlike feathery sprays at branch ends, reminding one of spiraea to which it is closely related. Both this species and ninebark (opposite) were originally described as being in the genus *Spiraea*.

    The young twigs are covered with short, soft hairs and the older branches are dark red, becoming, with age, gray. Its bark peels off in thin layers as in ninebark. The undersides of the coarsely toothed, small, oval leaves are covered with fine, white, velvety hairs. As with mountain ninebark, the dry, mature, feathery blooms and seeds remain on the plants into winter.

    The Pueblo Indians of New Mexico and the Cahuilla Indians of California ate the small, dry fruits of this, as well as other species of *Holodiscus*.

    It is considered edible for livestock use, but its palatability rates only from zero to fair, according to cattlemen.

    Where it grows on the coast it is known as ocean-spray.

145

Cerro Hawthorn

shinyleaf hawthorn, "thornapple"

Crataegus erythropoda

Rose family *(Rosaceae)*

Range: AZ, NM, CO; w. to CA; n. to Can.; e. to MI. Canyon streams, 4,500' - 8,000'.

This hawthorn may be identified by its coarsely toothed leaves and by its numerous shiny, dark red, nearly straight thorns up to 2 inches long. It is a rather small much-branched shrub (to about 9 feet) or a small tree (to about 20 feet) with reddish brown twigs.

Its small white flowers appear in April and May and occur in flat clusters. They are followed by red to dark brown to blackish fruits called haws which are about three-eighths of an inch in diameter. The haws remain on the plants into the winter unless they are first eaten by the numerous small birds and animals. Some people maintain that the fruits are most delicious when they are picked after having been frozen.

A hawthorn is the State flower of Missouri.

Acerola, the tiny applelike fruit of parsely-leaved hawthorn is richer in natural Vitamin C than any other fruit and is sold in most health food stores.

A Mexican species of hawthorn has crabapple-size fruits which are commonly sold, in season, in the native markets for immediate consumption or to be made into jelly or marmalade. Not only are the fruits good eating, but it is said that its plant parts such as roots can cure diabetes and even varicose veins.

River Hawthorn

Crataegus rivularis

Rose family *(Rosaceae)*

Range: Our whole range; w. to NV; n. to Can. Streambanks, 3,000' - 8,500'.

This hawthorn may be identified by its ovate, doubly toothed leaves; by few, glossy, blackish, curved thorns about 1 inch long; and by crimson to nearly black half-inch fruits which look like miniature apples.

Many Indian tribes ate the fruits, especially in times of food shortage, or dried and stored them for winter use, sometimes boiling them with cornmeal and forming the mass into cakes and drying them.

Of up to 900 species of hawthorn throughout the world, about 70 are native to the United States.

Hawthorns, for hundreds of years, have been favorite park and hedge plants in Europe, and in England its flowering branches were long used in May Day celebrations.

Many legends are connected with the hawthorn, the most interesting of which alleges that Joseph of Arimathea visited Britain and constructed the first church there, and from his staff sprang the Glastonbury hawthorn.

The word *Crataegus* is related to the Greek word for "strength" and was so named because of the great hardness of its wood, making it useful for such things as mill-wheel cogs, flails, mallets, hammer handles and blocks for wood engraving. Its roots are sometimes used as a substitute for briar in pipe making.

147

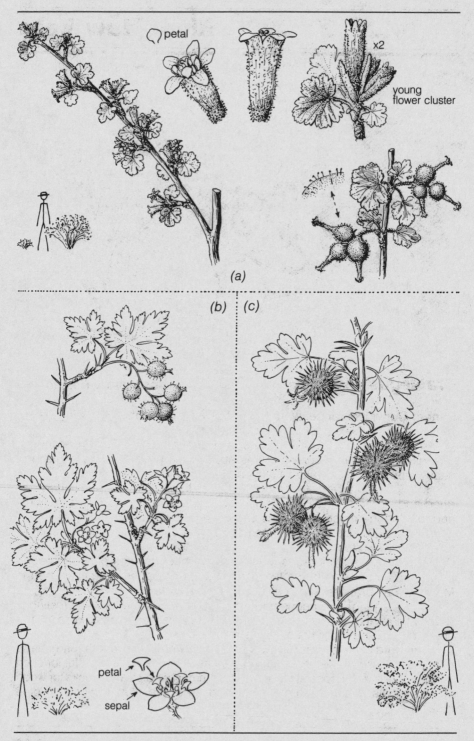

petal

x2

young
flower cluster

(a)

(b)

(c)

petal

sepal

148

Wax Currant

Ribes inebrians (a)

squaw currant, grosellero

Saxifrage family *(Saxifragaceae)*

Range: AZ, NM, CO, UT; w. to CA; n. to Can.; ne to NB & SD. Dry, sunny ridges & slopes, 3,500' - 11,000'.

Currants differ from gooseberries (below) in that they have no spines on their fruits or stems. The word "currant" comes from Middle English *raison of Coraunte* (raisin of Corinth) a Greek port from which currants were first introduced.

Wax currant forms rounded clumps from 2 to 4 feet high with much-branched, rigid stems. Its flowers consist of a white or pinkish, tubular calyx with very small white petals growing in its throat.

The sticky, crimson berries ripen in summer and can be eaten, but are rather tasteless. They are better used for making jelly. They are eaten by many birds and animals. Indians ate the berries, either fresh or dried, or crushed and pressed into cakes. They also used the berries for making an intoxicating beverage. It has been said that the flowers are better tasting than the fruits.

The fuzzy, somewhat sticky leaves are 3 to 5 lobed and were eaten by the Indians with deer fat (later with mutton fat).

Gooseberries

Mountain or Redfruited Gooseberry (b) gooseberry

currant, uva espín(a) [spiny grape], uva crespa [crisp-leaved grape]

Ribes montigenum

Saxifrage family *(Saxifragaceae)*

Range: AZ, NM, CO, UT; w. to CA; n. to Can. Exposed slopes & ridges, 7,000' - 11,500'.

A straggling, much-branched, spiny shrub from 1 to 2 feet high. The flowers are in groups of 3 to 7; sepals are petallike and greenish, fading to pink (p. 99); and the petals are smaller and greenish white to rose purple, and you have to look twice to find them.

The red berries are covered with sticky bristles and are edible, but not tasty. They are avidly eaten by birds. Both deer and livestock browse the plant.

Orange Gooseberry (c)

Ribes pinetorum

Range: AZ, NM. Well-drained soils, coniferous forests, 6,500' - 10,000'.

Slightly larger than the mountain, with more-spreading stems to 4 feet tall. The flowers are orange. Its berries are very spiny and at first, red, but purplish at maturity. They are edible but hard to eat on account of the spines. Its leaves are not deeply incised.

In England, gooseberries are very popular, both as a fresh dessert and in preserves.

Little Fendlerbush

Utah fendlerella

Fendlerella utahensis   Saxifrage family *(Saxifragaceae)*

Range: Our whole range; w. to CA; s. to Mex. Canyons & rocky cliffs, 4,500' - 8,000'.

 Mockorangelike flowers easily identify this 1 to 3 foot high shrub as being closely related to mockorange and false mockorange, differing from both in that it has 5 instead of 4 white petals. The blooms occur in few-flowered clusters at the ends of the leafy branches and appear from May into August.
 Somewhat shreddy bark occurs on the main stems, but the slender twigs are gray green due to the very short, stiff hairs that lie close against the stems. Its many, simple leaves are also hairy, oblong to elliptic and about ⅝ of an inch long and opposite (occasionally clustered in bundles on the older twigs).
 Blacktail and mule deer, bighorn sheep and domestic goats browse the bushes, and cattle in dire straits deign to feed upon it.
 Little fendlerbush is placed by some botanists in the hydrangea family. It was first collected near Kanab, Utah in 1873 as *Whipplea* to honor Lt. A. W. Whipple, U. S. Army Commander of the Pacific Railroad Expedition from the Mississippi River to Los Angeles in 1853 and 1854.

Roundleaf Buffaloberry

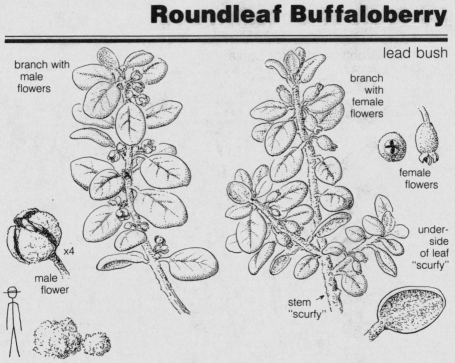

branch with male flowers

lead bush

branch with female flowers

female flowers

under-side of leaf "scurfy"

x4

male flower

stem "scurfy"

Shepherdia rotundifolia

Elaeagnus or Oleaster family
(*Elaeagnaceae*)

Range: n. AZ, s. UT, CO(?). Steep, rocky slopes, 5,000' - 8,000'.

Two of the three buffaloberries in the world are included in this book: one is described here, the other in the pinyon-juniper belt; the third is Canada buffaloberry, barely dipping into our range.

The shrub is from 3 to 4 feet high and has a gray green look as if it were sprayed silvery gray, but with green showing through.

The thick leaves are nearly round and covered with silvery to olive gray scales. They are cupped downward and their undersides are white woolly, besides being scaly.

Tiny, gray green flowers, appearing in May and June, do not have petals, but the calyx is flowerlike and covered with gray green scales. Male and female flowers are produced by separate plants. The female blossoms develop into small, olive-shaped fruits which are scaly and silvery woolly.

Its berries are eaten raw, but they taste better when made into jelly or cool, refreshing drinks (sugar helps!).

Quail, catbirds and thrashers, as well as bears, chipmunks and ground squirrels have been reported as eating the berries.

It receives one of its common names because the whole plant is silvery gray or lead colored.

Lanceleaf Cottonwood

smoothbark cottonwood (or poplar)

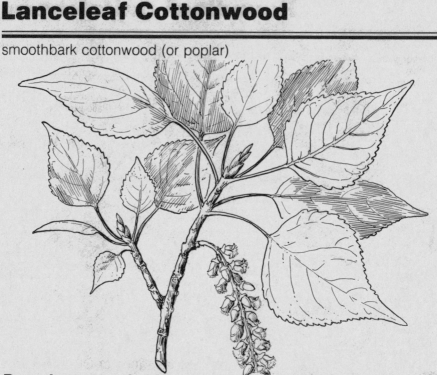

Populus acuminata

Willow family *(Salicaceae)*

Range: Our whole range (scattered); w. to CA; n. to Can. Along streams, 4,500' - 8,500'.

In size and shape, the leaves of this cottonwood are somewhere in between the extremes of narrowleaf (opposite) and plains (p. 91) cottonwoods and is considered by some botanists to be a cross between these two. Technically, then, the scientific name should be written *Populus* X *acuminata* indicating this crossbreeding.

This tree, growing about 50 feet tall by 2 feet in diameter, is more upright in form, has a broader, more spreading crown and has more white bark on the larger branches than narrowleaf cottonwood.

Pale yellow brown, often 4-angled, twigs separate this species from narrowleaf cottonwood which has yellow green to orange twigs.

Indians avidly sought the fresh young buds of spring as refreshing tidbits after their dreary winter diet. Cottonwood logs are still used by the Pueblo Indians to make their double-headed ceremonial drums, hollowed out by burning and scraping. The Hopi Indians use cottonwood roots from which to carve their Kachina dolls.

Cottonwood, along with aspen, is relished by beaver and porcupine alike. Several species of birds and small animals, as well as deer, elk and moose use either its buds and catkins or its bark, twigs and foliage as food.

Narrowleaf Cottonwood

black or mountain cottonwood; álamo

Populus angustifolia

Willow family *(Salicaceae)*

Range: Our whole range; w. to NV; n. to Can.; s. to Mex. Streambanks & valleys, 4,000' - 8,000'.

Willowlike, narrow leaves, yellow green in color above, but lighter beneath, identify this as the narrowleaf cottonwood (p. 98). Young cottonwoods, for this reason, are often mistaken for willows.

The earliest description of this cottonwood appears in the narrative of the Lewis and Clark Expedition, when, on June 6, 1805, on what is now the Teton River, it was reported "...a species of cottonwood with a leaf like that of the Wild Cherry."

Similar to lanceleaf cottonwood (opposite), it is a medium-size tree 50 to 60 feet tall and 12 to 20 inches through, averaging more like 40 feet in height and 16 inches in diameter. Its crown is less spreading than the tops of other cottonwoods.

Round, greenish twigs differentiate narrowleaf from lanceleaf cottonwood. This species is usually planted as a shade tree in towns and around dwellings, and is used for fuel and fenceposts; rarely for lumber.

Indians used the young shoots for basketry in a manner similar to that in which willow osiers were used. Montana Indians considered its inner bark good for preventing scurvy.

Coyote Willow

gray, sandbar, slender, basket, acequia or narrowleaf willow

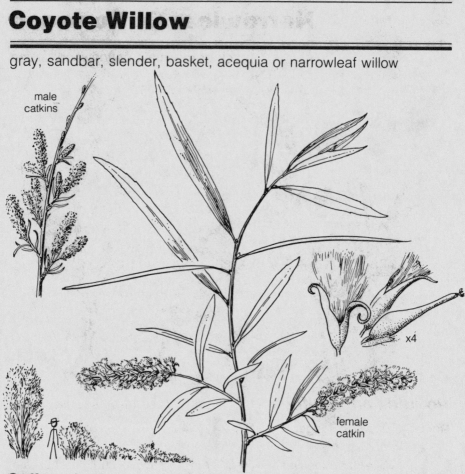

male catkins

x4

female catkin

Salix exigua

Willow family *(Salicaceae)*

Range: Our whole range; w. to CA; n. to Can.; e. to NB; s. to Mex. Streambanks, lakeshores & irrigation ditches, 4,000' - 9,500'.

The common shrubby willow of this belt grows in thickets anywhere ground water is abundant and near the surface.

At most, 15 feet tall, but much smaller where cropped by wildlife and livestock. Its older stems are ashy gray with newer twigs reddish. The long and narrow leaves are, at first, silvery, due to fine hairs; later, as the hairs wear off, the leaves become dull grayish green, but remain silvery on their undersides. The leaf margins are minutely toothed.

Wherever this little willow abounds, Indians use its slender twigs (osiers) for baskets; moreover, willow twigs are probably more generally used than any other material, as they are favored the world over for basketry construction. In the folklore of many countries willows are sacred trees.

Red-osier Dogwood

American dogwood, "kinnikinnick"

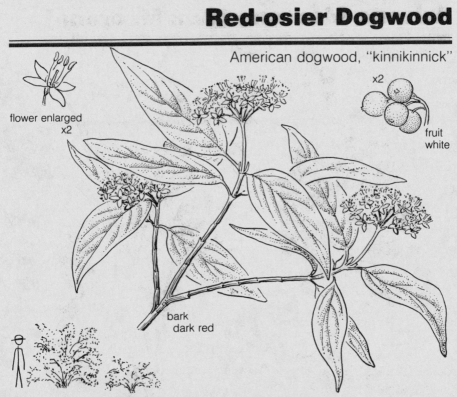

flower enlarged
x2

x2

fruit
white

bark
dark red

Cornus stolonifera

Dogwood family *(Cornaceae)*

Range: Our whole range; w. to CA; n. to AK; e. to Nfld & VA; s. to Mex. Along streams, in swampy areas, hills, slopes & banks, 4,500' - 10,000'.

This dogwood is easily recognized by its bark: it is bright red, hence the "red" in red-osier. It is called "osier" because its slim, pliable stems resemble those of the osier (willow) and were used for basketry.

Red-osier dogwood is a medium-size shrub, growing usually from 3 to 6 feet tall. Its long red branches bend to the ground and take root wherever they touch, sending up new clumps of stems.

The flowers grow in clusters, are tiny and white (p. 98) and produce pea-size, lead-colored or dull white fruits. Linnaeus, originator of our system of taxonomic classification, liked a dessert made by the Lapps of dogwood berries.

"Kinnikinnick" is a word of Algonquian origin and simply means "mixture." Mixtures of dried leaves and/or bark of the red-osier dogwood, as well as of sumac, willow and bearberry were all used by the Indians and pioneers as a substitute for tobacco, or sometimes mixed with it. Red-osier leaves and inner bark, when smoked, are reported to have a slight narcotic effect which could be harmful.

Arizona Madrone [Sp.: Madroño]

Arizona arbute

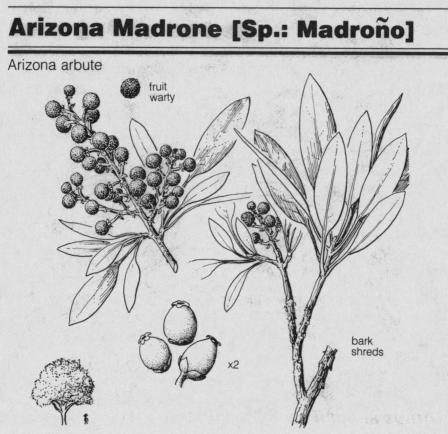

fruit
warty

x2

bark
shreds

Arbutus arizonica

Heather family *(Ericaceae)*

Range: Of limited distribution in the mountains of extreme se AZ & sw NM; s. to Mex. Well-drained, gravelly, sunny sites, 4,000' - 8,000'.

Madrone is a member of the heather family, along with myrtle blueberry and bearberry. Other members of the family include huckleberry, azalea, rhododendron, heather, manzanita, cranberry and trailing arbutus (May-flower).

This tree is evergreen, growing from 15 to 45 feet tall and from 18 to 24 inches in diameter. The bark of the main trunk is grayish and scaly, peeling off in papery sheets, but on young stems and twigs it is dark red, peeling off in long, thin scales. The 1½ to 3 inch long leaves are about ½ to 1 inch wide, glossy, leathery and light green above, but paler beneath. The contrast between the grayish bark, the red twigs and the pale green leaves makes a very pleasing combination.

Its urn-shaped, flesh-colored to white flowers occur in loose clusters at branch ends and can be found on the tree from April to September. The warty berries are about pea size and brilliant orange red.

Fir-Aspen Belt

(Approx. 8,000' - 9,500' elev.)

Here, in the midsections of the mountains, this belt has a much different aspect from the pine-oak belt below. The landscape changes from the open-spaced ponderosa pine groves to denser stands of Douglas-fir, due mainly to additional available moisture. Annual precipitation as one proceeds up the mountainsides increases as each belt is reached, and is now nearly double that of the pinyon-juniper belt. This greater precipitation makes for an abundance of vegetation and hence more material to make rich, black humus to support still more vegetation. Annual precipitation has now increased to somewhere between 25 and 30 inches.

As one ascends, winds become stronger, therefore the dense stands of Douglas-fir and aspen growing close together (p. 103) receive mutual protection from their own kind, thus acting as windbreaks against toppling in the high winds.

Here sunlight rarely reaches the forest floor, though occasionally the sylvan scene is interspersed by grasslands, called parks.

The quaking aspen with its white bark is set off against the dark green of the Douglas-fir, and occupies the soils with greater moisture content. At the lower edges of this belt, plants from the pine-oak belt such as Rocky Mountain juniper, a serviceberry and two species of snowberries may be found. On the south-facing slopes, ponderosa pine and Douglas-fir occur together. Interfingering the upper edges of this belt will be found plants from the spruce-fir forest above. They are such plants as Engelmann and blue spruce, subalpine fir and currant.

Only shrubs and trees that can tolerate the reduced shade produced by the fir and aspen groves can survive here. Such plants, among others, are kinnikinnick, honeysuckle, raspberry, thimbleberry and mountain-ash.

Two other conifers are found within this belt as well: common juniper and white fir. Streamsides are lined with willows, and Alpine clematis clambers over the shrubs and trees.

Occasionally pure stands of lodgepole pine may be encountered within the Douglas-fir forest. They occur where fire has swept through the Douglas-firs, and lodgepole pine then becomes the "pioneer" tree; that is, the first tree to revegetate a burned-over area. Aspen frequently grows in clearings created by forest fires, and are also considered "pioneer" trees.

There are only 17 species listed for this belt; however nearly twice as many plants push upward from the belts below, plus about 10 species that wander downward from the spruce-fir belt above.

Douglas-fir

Douglas-, yellow, red or false spruce; yellow or red fir; Douglastree, "Oregon-pine"

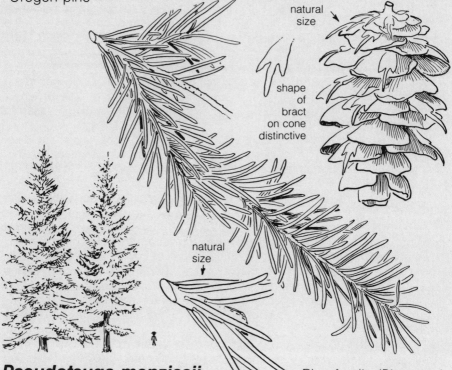

natural size

shape of bract on cone distinctive

natural size

Pseudotsuga menziesii
Pine family *(Pinaceae)*

Range: Our whole range; w. to CA; n. to AK; s. to Mex. Deep soils, 4,000' - 11,000'.

Douglas-fir is not a true fir, nor is it a hemlock, although its scientific name translates "false hemlock."

"Mouse-tails" sticking out from between the cone scales give its cones a distinctive fringed appearance entirely different from any other cone (p. 105). It is also distinguished from the true firs because its cones hang down and fall off whole, in contrast to the firs whose cones are upright and disintegrate when mature.

Its needles are blunt, flat, flexible and grooved above.

In our area it grows to about 130 feet, but on the coast it reaches a height of over 300 feet.

It is highly regarded for lumber and is prized for Christmas trees. The twigs and needles of this tree were once used as a coffee substitute.

It is the State tree of Oregon.

trembling, golden or mountain aspen (poplar or asp); quaky, popple, álamo blanco [white poplar], alamillo, chopo tremblón [trembling poplar]

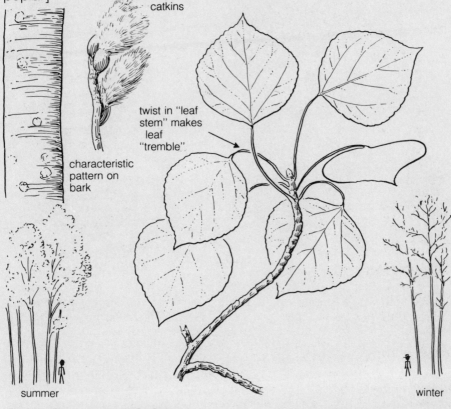

catkins

twist in "leaf stem" makes leaf "tremble".

characteristic pattern on bark

summer   winter

Populus tremuloides   Willow family *(Salicaceae)*

Range: Our whole range; w. to CA; n. to the Arctic Circle, thence across Can. to Lab.; across n. U.S. from WA to NJ, incl. MO & NB; s. to Mex. Moist, sandy soils, 6,000' - 11,500'.

There is no mistaking these trees in the fall — their dense groves turn brilliant golden and stand out vividly for acre upon acre against the green mountainsides (p. 100). At other times of the year there is also no mistaking its white-barked trunks (p. 101), even in the dead of winter when its branches are bare. Its leaves, too, are a give-away: the leaf stems are flattened lengthwise, so that the leaves constantly flutter, even in the slightest breeze.

Its bark is the favorite food of the beaver, who, after removing it, uses the twigs and trunks for building his dam and lodge.

White Fir

balsam or silver fir; white balsam, pino real blanco [true white "pine"]

cone scale

seeds
winged

upper
branches or
older trees

lower
branches

Abies concolor

Pine family *(Pinaceae)*

Range: Our whole range; w. to CA; n. to Can.; s. to Mex. Moist, well-drained soils, 5,500' - 7,000' in canyons; 8,000' - 11,500' on n. slopes.

White fir is one of the most beautiful trees in North America. Because of this it is often planted as an ornamental. It produces a silvery blue green dense, conical crown. When mature, it is about 80 to 100 feet tall in this region, with trunks normally about 2 to 3 feet thick and densely clothed with branches nearly to the ground. It is highly prized for Christmas trees — millions are grown commercially and harvested annually.

The bluish green, aromatic needles are unusually long for a fir, often 2 or more inches in length and curved, in contrast to the 1 inch long needles of the subalpine fir. Typical of the true firs, when the 3 to 5 inch cones mature in September or October, the scales drop off, leaving an upright spikelike central stalk — a distinguishing feature even in midwinter. The bark of young trees is smooth and gray and broken by blisters of resin or "balsam," hence one of its common names: balsam fir. The bark of old trees is ashy gray and deeply furrowed.

White fir grows at lower elevations than subalpine fir, and is often found on hillsides with ponderosa pine and Douglas-fir, and in canyons with blue spruce.

The wood makes a second-grade lumber.

The seeds are eaten by grouse, chipmunks, squirrels and deer.

Common Juniper

dwarf, low, mountain, Alpine, prostrate or Siberian juniper; ground "cedar;" enebro

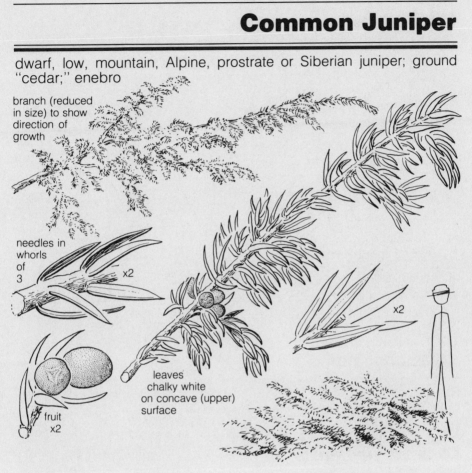

branch (reduced in size) to show direction of growth

needles in whorls of 3   x2

fruit x2

leaves chalky white on concave (upper) surface

x2

Juniperus communis   Cypress family *(Cupressaceae)*

Range: AZ, NM, CO, UT; w. to CA; e. to NC; n. to AK; thence across Can. to Gnld; circumpolar to Eu. & Asia. Dry, open, rocky mountainsides, sometimes in partial shade, 5,000' - 10,000'.

This, the most widely distributed juniper of the western hemisphere, can be readily separated from all others: it is the only juniper in our range that is shrubby. It forms dense mats 3 to 10 feet in diameter, its plumelike branchlets usually rising no more than 3 feet above the ground. The needles are also distinctive — they are awl shaped, in groups of 3, rather prickly, and stand out from the stems, allowing its reddish brown, scaly bark to be seen.

The dark blue, juicy, pea-size fruits (p. 96) ripen in late summer and are whitened with a "bloom." These pungent berries are used to flavor gin.

Incidentally, from the Latin *iuniperus,* through Old French, *genèvre* and Dutch *genever,* comes, through shortening, our word "gin."

Utah Honeysuckle

red twinberry

fruit
red

Lonicera utahensis   Honeysuckle family *(Caprifoliaceae)*

Range: AZ, NM, CO(?), UT; w. to CA; n. to Can. Moist soils, open coniferous forests, 8,000' - 11,000'.

This species has white to creamy, trumpet-shaped flowers in pairs and a bright red, pea-size, double berry, one usually larger than the other. The leaves are pale green but whitish beneath, and from 1 to 2½ inches long.

It is a 2 to 5 foot high shrub.

In spite of the berries being considered inedible for humans (they are reported to be poisonous), they are eaten by birds and chipmunks.

Its flowers are sometimes pulled and sucked for the rich nectar that they contain.

In Europe, the flowers of an Old World species are sometimes used for making perfume, and the fruits for making a syrup used in the treatment of asthma.

The fruits of all species of honeysuckles are said to induce vomiting and purgation.

Bearberry Honeysuckle

black twinberry, involucred honeysuckle, skunkberry, madreselva

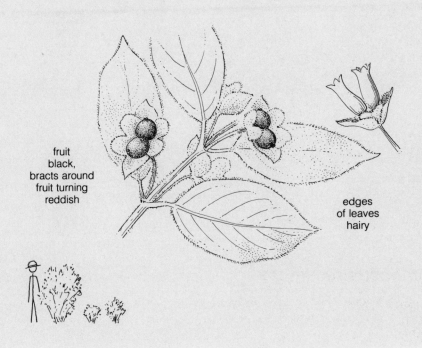

fruit
black,
bracts around
fruit turning
reddish

edges
of leaves
hairy

Lonicera involucrata   Honeysuckle family *(Caprifoliaceae)*

Range: AZ, NM, CO, UT; w. to CA; n. to AK; ne to MI; e. across Can.; s. to Mex. Moist soils, forests and streamsides, 7,500' - 11,500'.

This species has large, showy, purplish red, leaflike bracts, yellow twin flowers about 1 inch long, and shiny purple black twin fruits. The leaves are bright green, glandular dotted and hairy and from 2 to 5 inches long. It grows 2 to 7 feet tall.

Although considered unpalatable by white man (they are tart and sour, but can be eaten in an emergency), several Indian tribes ate the fruits fresh, or dried and stored them for winter use.

The juicy fruits which ripen in August and September, are eaten by a variety of birds and small animals, as chipmunks, as well as by bears.

The tubular flowers are very attractive to hummingbirds.

163

Redberried Elder (-berry)

red, scarlet or bunchberry elder(-berry)

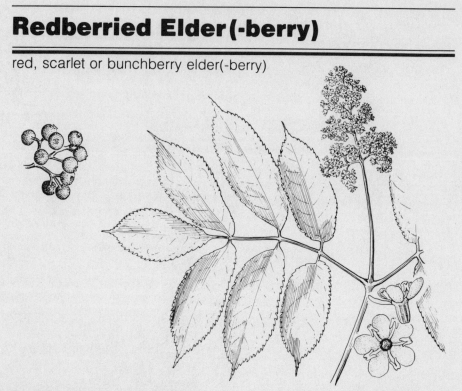

Sambucus racemosa Honeysuckle family *(Caprifoliaceae)*

Range: AZ, NM, CO, UT; w. to CA; n. to AK; e. across U.S. & Can. to GA, MI & Nfld; also Eu. & Asia. Moist places in woods, especially streambanks, 5,000' - 12,000'.

    This elder, or elderberry, shrub has showy, pyramidal clusters of small, fragrant creamy white blossoms followed by strikingly beautiful, shiny, scarlet berries. The flowers appear in late spring; the fruit in late summer. Various sources report this species as poisonous; however, Indians ate the berries raw or boiled or made a tea from its roots without apparent ill effects. Jellies, pies and wine are sometimes made from the seedy berries.

    Numerous birds and small animals use the berries as a source of food, while moose and deer browse the twigs and foliage.

    Growing to about 5 feet tall, this elder usually has 5 to 7 thin leaflets on each leaf stalk. They have sharply serrated edges and are dark green and smooth on their upper surfaces, but are soft hairy on the reverse side. The bark is greenish brown to gray brown and smooth, but older stems have raised, warty spots. The young twigs are covered with a fine hair.

    The Indians hollowed out the pithy stems to make flutes.

    CAUTION: Children have been poisoned by making blowguns, whistles and the like from the stalks and placing them in their mouths.

Arizona Mountain-ash

serbo, serbal de cazadores [hunters]

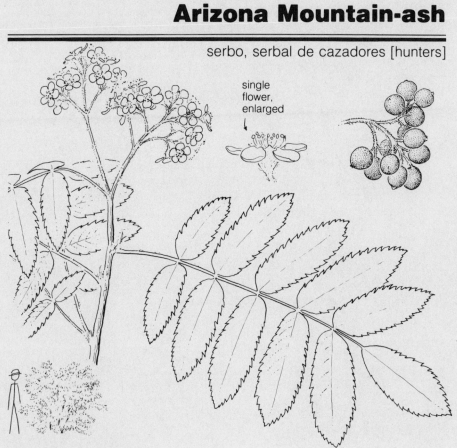

single flower, enlarged

Sorbus dumosa

Rose family *(Rosaceae)*

Range: ne AZ, sw NM. Sandy or gravelly, moist soils, 7,500' - 10,000'.

This mountain-ash is an attractive shrub or small tree, growing from 3 to 10 feet tall, but usually no higher than 7 feet. Its dull green leaves are divided into numerous (5 to 13) sharp-toothed leaflets that much resemble rose leaves. Their undersides are a paler green.

Small white flowers grow in flat-topped clusters at branch ends and bloom in June and July. The orange red berries follow in early fall and are relished by a number of species of wildlife. They are also eaten by people, but if *you* try them, *be sure that they are fully ripe!*

The young twigs vary from tan to reddish and are densely white hairy. As they grow older, they lose the hairs and become smooth and reddish brown to gray.

In the Old World, bits of mountain-ash wood were used as charms to avert almost any disaster.

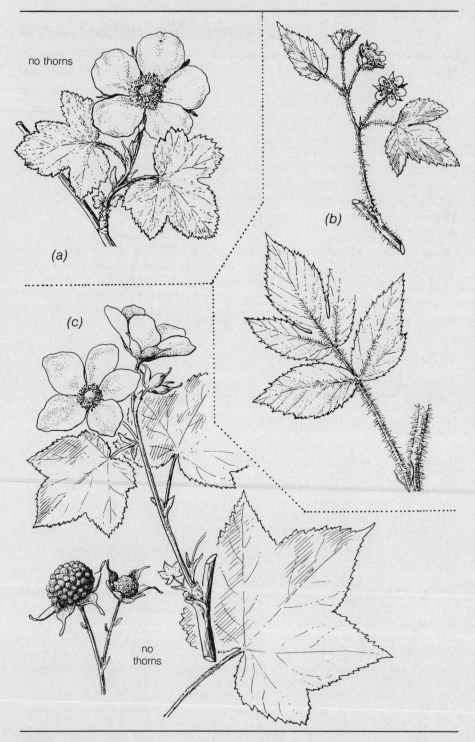

no thorns

(a)

(b)

(c)

no
thorns

Raspberry, Thimbleberry

Rubus species
Rose family *(Rosaceae)*

Of the numerous groups in the rose family, this one seems to be the most difficult to classify. There is such a diversity of opinion that from half a hundred to nearly 400 species of *Rubus* have been recorded, making positive identification rather difficult — truly a "brierpatch."

The so-called "berry" is really a cluster of many diminutive, fleshy, 1-seeded fruits. In thimbleberries and raspberries, the whole cluster slips off in one piece, thimblelike, but in blackberries, the small fruits fall off singly.

All of the fruits are good to eat. Tasty jams, jellies, pies, tarts and wines are made from them.

New Mexican Raspberry *(a)*
Rubus neomexicanus
frambueso
Range: s. AZ, sw NM; s. to Mex. Moist, open woods & slopes, 5,000 - 9,000'.

This species grows to a height of about 5 feet, but occasionally reaches up to 9 feet. One or 2 white flowers are borne on short, leafy, lateral branches. Its juicy, red fruits are eaten by humans, birds and animals alike. The leaves are thinly hairy on the upper surfaces and downy on the undersides. The young twigs are slender and smooth, but the old bark flakes off.

Deer browse the shrub to some extent.

Wild Red Raspberry *(b)*

Rubus idaeus
western red raspberry, zarzaidea [Mt. Ida bramble], mata espinosa [spiny shrub] (usually reserved for blackberry)

Range: AZ, NM, CO, UT; w. to CA; n. to AK; across n. U. S. & Can. to NC & Nfld; Eu. & Asia. Often in dry locations & open slopes, 7,000' - 11,500'.

A very prickly shrub to about 4 or 5 feet tall with flexible "canes" (woody stems). The almost inconspicuous white flower petals are nearly hidden among the sepals. They produce the tastiest-of-all red fruits which are picked in abundance, if the bears don't get there first! Compound, dark green leaves are made up of 3- to 5-toothed leaflets that are downy white to downy gray below. The bark is reddish brown underneath the multitudinous prickles.

The Indians ate the fruits fresh or dried them for later use. Its shoots were peeled and eaten and the leaves and twigs made into a tea.

Western Thimbleberry *(c)*
Rubus parviflorus
white-flowering raspberry, thimble raspberry, salmonberry

Range: AZ, NM, CO; w. to CA; n. to AK; ne to MI. Very irregularly distributed, canyons & wooded slopes, 8,000' - 9,500'.

The largest flowered of our three species (p. 102), even though its Latin name means "small-flowered." It grows usually to about 3 feet high, but some plants reach up to 5 feet. Its red, squatty, thimble-shaped fruit is the least tasty of all, but edible. The Indians ate the fruits with salmon eggs, accounting for one of the common names.

The berries are relished by most birds and animals.

Mountain Lover

myrtle pachystima, mountain hedge, mountain myrtle, Oregon box-wood, myrtle boxleaf

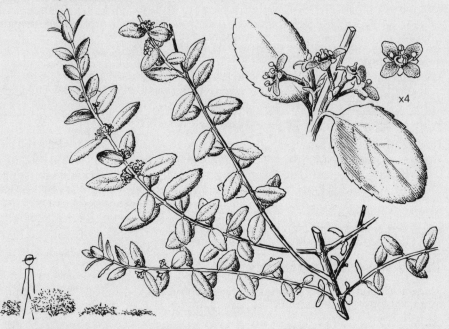

x4

Pachystima myrsinites   Bittersweet family *(Celastraceae)*

Range: AZ, NM, CO, UT; w. to CA; n. to Can. Deep forests under shrubs & trees, 6,000' - 10,000'.

Mountain lover is truly named — it is found almost nowhere else except in high mountain forests. It especially loves shady places under shrubs and trees where it is moist.

It is a low (no more than 2 feet high), spreading, evergreen shrub with small, oval, thick leaves with slightly toothed edges. To some they are reminiscent of the "boxwood" found in formal gardens.

The minute (1/8 to 1/6 inch wide), almost inconspicuous, 4-petalled flowers are red brown and found in the leaf axils, but you have to look for them as they are nearly hidden by the leaves (p. 102). They appear in May and produce inconspicuous seed capsules.

Mountain lover has been adapted for rock gardens, making a nice evergreen shrub if it is grown in half-shady, moist places.

It seems odd that such a small shrub with such tiny flowers should have so many common names. The family is sometimes called stafftree or burning-bush.

Kinnikinnick

bearberry, sandberry, chipmunk apples, manzanita

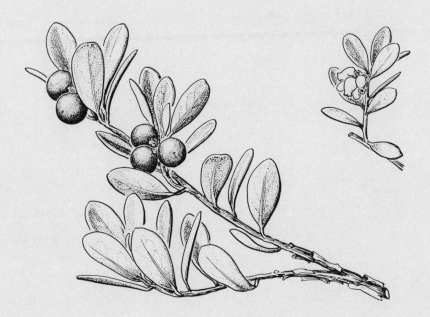

Arctostaphylos uva-ursi

Heather family *(Ericaceae)*

Range: AZ(?), NM, CO, UT; w. to CA; e. to Atl. Coast; n. to AK & Gnld., thence around the world through Eu. & Asia. Rocky places, in sandy soil on shaded slopes, 6,000' - 10,000'.

A low, trailing, evergreen shrub with long, flexible, woody stems which root at the joints where they touch the ground, sometimes completely carpeting a wide area. The branch ends upturn for no more than 12 inches. The bark of the main stems is reddish and shreddy.

The small, abundant leaves are leathery and quite shiny green on the upper surfaces. The Indians used the leaves to make tea, and the pioneers for treating urinary disorders. The Indians have long used the leaves as a substitute for, or mixed with, tobacco.

Waxy, pink-tinged, white flowers droop from the stems like so many tiny, upsidedown urns, blooming from May through June. The red berries (p. 102) which ripen in the fall are rather attractive.

The berries are supposedly relished by bears as well as other Upland dwellers, especially grouse.

Alpine Clematis

Rocky Mountain clematis

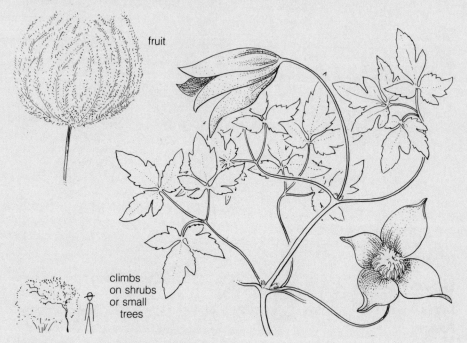

fruit

climbs
on shrubs
or small
trees

Clematis pseudoalpina   Buttercup family *(Ranunculaceae)*

Range: AZ, NM, CO, UT; n. to MT; ne to SD. Moist woods, 6,000' - 10,000'.

A somewhat smaller woody vine than its cousin in the pinyon-juniper belt, but nevertheless its feathery clusters of long, silky seed plumes immediately identify this attractive vine in the fall.

It usually is not much over 5 feet long, and does not "sprawl" like the virgin's-bower, but rather clambers, vinelike, over shrubs and small trees. As with other clematises, it does not have petals as such, but has showy petallike sepals. The flower colors can range from blue to purple, violet or lavender (rarely white).

The long, fluffy plumes, aided greatly by the wind, help to distribute, over long distances, the seeds to which they are attached.

Boy Scouts have been known to use the fluffy seed plumes as tinder for starting fires by the "fire-by-friction" method.

Clematis, along with such other plants as anemone, columbine, larkspur, peony and ranunculus, belongs to the buttercup family, the oldest known family, from a geological standpoint, of flowering plants. About 150 species of clematis are found throughout the world. The preferred pronunciation is KLEM-uh-tiss; however klih-MAT-iss, klih-MATE-iss and klih-MAH-tiss are also heard.

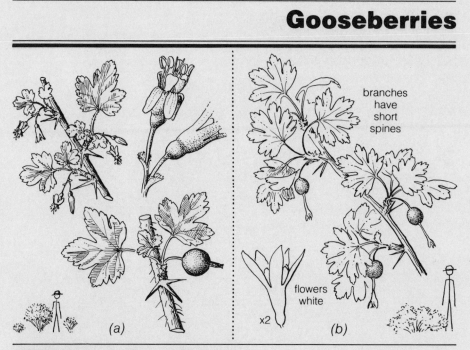

branches have short spines

flowers white

x2

(a)   *(b)*

Whitestem Gooseberry *(a)*

Ribes inerme   wine gooseberry   Saxifrage family *(Saxifragaceae)*

Range: AZ, NM, CO, UT; w. to CA; n. to Can. Moist, shady places, 5,000' - 11,000'.

This species grows usually no more than 3 feet tall with smooth, slender, whitish stems, later turning to red brown and becoming flaky. Where the leaves join the stem it may have a few short spines, but usually it is unarmed. One to 3 bell-shaped flowers appear in the leaf axils, the calyx being greenish to purplish and obvious — the petals, hidden in the calyx tube, are small and pinkish to white.

The fruits are wine colored or nearly black, and tart, but edible.

Trumpet Gooseberry *(b)*

Ribes leptanthum

Range: Our whole range. Dry, sunny places, 5,500' - 12,000'.

This species is usually 3 feet tall (occasionally to 6 feet). Its young shoots are very spiny, with from 1 to 3 long spines in the leaf axils (where the leaves join the stem). One or 2 flowers composed of greenish white, tubular calyxes contain small whitish to pinkish, almost hidden petals. The blackish, lustrous berry is edible.

As with most gooseberries (and currants, too), the berries were eaten either fresh or dried for later use by the Indians.

Birds also eat the fruits, and deer as well as domestic animals browse the foliage.

171

Scouler Willow

black, fire, mountain willow

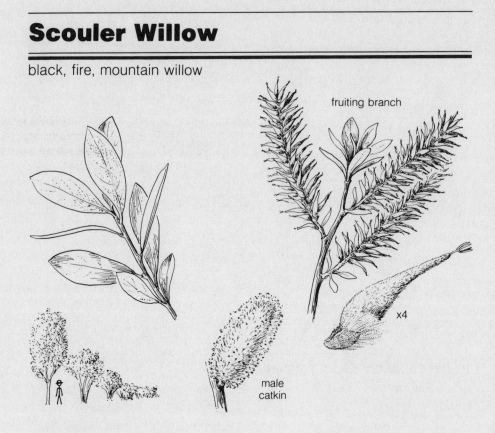

fruiting branch

x4

male catkin

Salix scouleriana

Willow family *(Salicaceae)*

Range: Our whole range; w. to CA; n. to AK; ne to SD. Moist places, 6,500' - 11,000'.

A medium-tall, thicket-forming willow, sometimes treelike with a single trunk. Generally found in moist places, but often grows on apparently dry ground with fir, spruce and pine. Its gray brown to blackish bark is divided into broad, flat ridges. Its twigs are reddish orange to dull yellow and are dotted with a few corky spots.

Scouler willow leaves differ from most willow leaves in that they are wider at their tips than at their bases and *are not* toothed. Their upper surfaces are dark green and shiny, while their lower, heavily veined surfaces are usually densely covered with reddish hairs.

The exceptionally large oval catkins (male), which appear before the leaves, are quite conspicuous in May and early June when they are yellow with pollen. The female flowers produce the fuzzy catkins.

Mule deer and livestock browse its foliage and young twigs, so much so, in fact, that often by early spring only stubble remains.

Spruce-Fir Belt

This is the highest, wettest, windiest and coldest of all the belts in which full-size trees can grow. In contrast to the fir-aspen belt immediately below, the trees of this belt are usually smaller, occupying streambanks and meadow edges; growing in tight clumps of several mature trees surrounded by younger saplings; or are found in more open locations. Here the heaviest snowfall of any of the mountain belts is encountered; in fact, twice as much snow falls here as in the fir-aspen belt below. Because of this, most of the Southwest's ski areas are located on these parts of the mountains in order to take advantage of the deep, powdery snow. Annual precipitation is 30 to 90, or more, inches.

The shade of the forest, together with lower temperatures, causes the snow to stay on the ground late into spring and sometimes well into summer. It melts gradually, thus assuring the vegetation a continuing supply of water throughout the short growing season of no more than 100 to 120 days.

In this belt grow the two key species of trees — the sharp-needled Engelmann spruce with hanging cones (p. 104), and the soft-needled sub-alpine fir with upright cones (p. 105). Spruce is the larger and more abundant of the two. Together they form the climax forest of this belt.

Also found here are other shrubs and trees: waxflower, Wolf's currant, Bebb willow, myrtle blueberry, blue spruce and lodgepole, bristlecone and limber pines. A variety of limber pine — Mexican white — also occurs in this belt in southern Arizona and New Mexico as well as in west Texas.

Where fires have burned over the forests, grow stands of pure lodgepole pines. Toward the upper reaches of this belt, vegetation becomes progressively smaller until treeline is reached. There it is stunted and dwarfed because of high winds and other adverse conditions.

This belt has also been called the Hudsonian Zone because of similarities with the flora (and fauna) of the region around Hudson Bay in east-central Canada. It is sometimes called the Subalpine Zone, as it occurs just below the zone which contains Alpine-type plants.

In addition to the 12 species listed for this belt, 35 plants reach up into this belt from below.

Engelmann Spruce Key Species

mountain, silver or "white" spruce

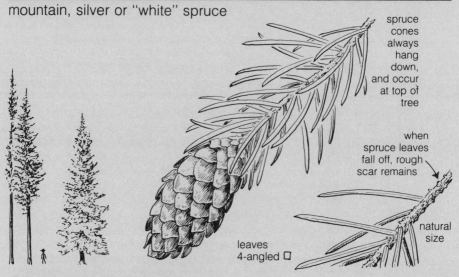

spruce cones always hang down, and occur at top of tree

when spruce leaves fall off, rough scar remains

natural size

leaves 4-angled ▫

Picea engelmannii Pine family (Pinaceae)

Range: AZ, NM, CO, UT (scattered); w. to CA; n. to Can. Deep, moist soils, 8,000' - 11,500'.

Any time that you see this tree, together with subalpine fir (opposite), you are probably in the spruce-fir belt between 9,500 and 11,500 feet in elevation. These two trees are indicators of a climax forest — a stable and self-perpetuating forest community. The Engelmann spruce, as well as the subalpine fir, however, grow lower in the fir-aspen belt, too, especially on moist north-facing slopes and in canyons.

This species of spruce grows to be a well-formed tree up to 100 feet tall and with a diameter of about 3 feet. It has a dense, narrow, spirelike crown, often bearing masses of pendant cones (p. 104) on the topmost branches (in contrast to the upright cones of the fir). Another distinguishing feature of the cones is their rather small, flexible, papery cone scales. Because the cones do not fall apart like those of the subalpine fir, they may be found carpeting the ground beneath the trees.

At treeline, Engelmann spruce may become matted (p. 108) or bannerlike (p. 108).

Engelmann spruce is much in demand for Christmas trees. Spruce beer was sometimes made from its needles and twigs and taken to prevent scurvy. It was first allowed to ferment. It is one of the Navajos' favorite trees for ceremonial purposes, and is used for hoops, collars, bows, etc. It was used in their sweathouses much as we use oil of eucalyptus in our saunas.

Its wood is soft and weak and of limited usefulness as lumber.

174

Subalpine Fir

Alpine fir, "balsam" fir, "white" fir, "balsam," pino real, blanco de las sierras [mountain white (fir)]

Abies lasiocarpa

Pine family *(Pinaceae)*

Range: AZ, NM, CO, UT (scattered); w. to CA; n. to AK. Deep, moist soils, 7,000' - 11,500'.

Smallest of all the true firs, subalpine fir, true to its name, grows at an elevation higher than any other. It is readily identified by its dark purple cones standing upright in the very tops of the trees (p. 105). The cones are often decorated with crystalline globules of pitch, which, in warm weather, drip silvery droplets. At maturity, the cones fall apart, leaving a vertical peg which skiers notice even in the dead of winter.

The tree itself is slender and spirelike (p. 106) reaching a height of 40 to 60 feet, with a trunk diameter of no more than about 2 feet. It has short, dense, rigid branches, reaching out horizontally, giving it a shelflike appearance. Feel its needles — they are flexible, soft, flat and blunt (not sharp like spruce). They curve upward, as do the needles of white fir, but they are only one inch long, in contrast to the white fir's two-plus inches. The bark on young trees is light gray and smooth, except for resin blisters; on old trees it is gray to grayish brown, shallowly fissured and with cinnamon red scales.

The trees are usually found in cool, moist sites: at edges of alpine meadows, along streams and in wet ground.

Its seeds are eaten by birds and animals alike; mountain sheep and deer browse the foliage and twigs.

175

Corkbark Fir

Arizona fir

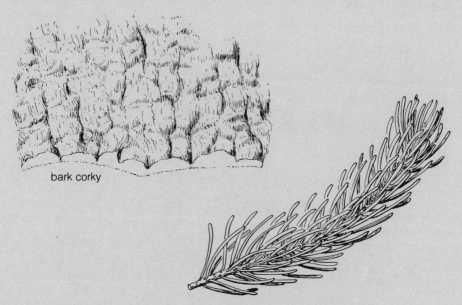

bark corky

Abies lasiocarpa **var.** *arizonica*   Pine family *(Pinaceae)*

Range: c. & se AZ, n. & sw NM, s. CO. Gravelly or rocky soils, 7,000' - 11,500'.

Corkbark fir is but a variety of, and intergrades with, subalpine fir (preceding page). Its needles and cones are similar and general growth is much the same; however, corkbark fir can be easily distinguished from subalpine fir by the soft, spongy bark which is cream colored or ashy gray.

The cones are generally longer and narrower than those of its near relative. As with the white and subalpine firs, it sheds its cone scales when the cones mature in September and October, leaving a spikelike central stalk standing upright on the uppermost branchlets.

It is interspersed with subalpine fir within its range; however, in some locations is may replace it completely.

Its needles are often as blue as those of Colorado blue spruce.

Because of the attractive, showy bark, it is highly valued as an ornamental tree and is planted extensively.

It was originally described in 1896 as a separate species; however, further study two years later proved it to be only a variety of subalpine fir. It was first discovered on the western slopes of the San Francisco Mountains near Flagstaff, Arizona.

Blue Spruce

Colorado blue spruce, silver spruce

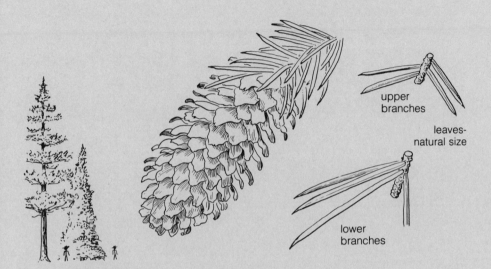

upper
branches

leaves-
natural size

lower
branches

Picea pungens   Pine family *(Pinaceae)*

Range: Our whole range (scattered); n. to MT & ID. Moist soils, 8,000' - 11,500'.

This spruce and Engelmann spruce (p. 174) are hard to tell apart; however, blue spruce cones are usually over 3 inches long, those of the Engelmann, usually about 2 inches long. If there are no cones on the trees, look at their barks — on mature blue it is pale to dark gray and furrowed; on Engelmann it is cinnamon red to purple brown and scaly.

The needles of blue spruce are generally longer, stiffer, sharper and more silvery than those of Engelmann spruce. It's easy to tell spruces from firs because their cones, which mature in August, are pendant and their needles sharp (firs have erect cones and "furry" needles).

Blue spruce has been called the most beautiful of all the evergreens, especially in its silvery form, and for this reason it is a highly prized ornamental and probably the most widely known of all the conifers. (A dozen horticultural varieties have been developed).

Blue spruce is the State tree of both Colorado and Utah, and is much in demand for Christmas trees.

"Turnbackers" from the "Pikes Peak or Bust" gold rush returned home with "silver" spruce instead of gold, transplanting it throughout the Midwest where it is still much in evidence.

177

Limber Pine

Rocky Mountain white pine, limbertwig

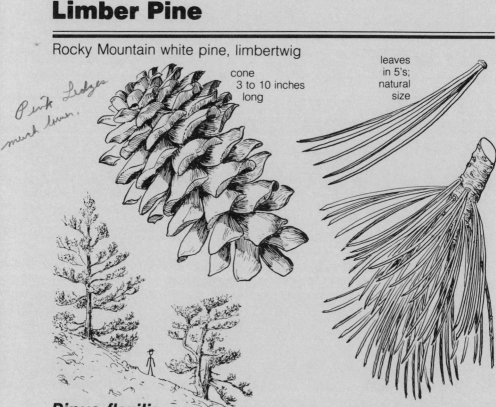

cone
3 to 10 inches
long

leaves
in 5's;
natural
size

*Pink Ledges
much lower.*

Pinus flexilis

Pine family *(Pinaceae)*

Range: Scattered throughout our range; w. to CA; n. to Can.; e. to SD & NB; s. to Mex. Dry, rocky, windswept slopes, 7,500' - 12,000'.

This pine is commonly found in the high mountains near treeline (p. 107). It can be differentiated from the bristlecone pine (p. 105) by its needles which are bunched at the ends of the twigs rather than growing all along the length of the branchlets as in bristlecone. Well-named because its branches are so limber that they can often be bent double without breaking, a distinct advantage in withstanding severe winds and snow loads. Another distinguishing feature is that the bark on old limber pines is dark brown to nearly black, while the bark of bristlecone pine is reddish brown. Limber pine may also be separated from the bristlecone by the color of their mature cones: in limber they are light brown and without prickles; in bristlecone, a deep brown purple and with prickles.

Ground and red squirrels, chipmunks, pinyon jays and magpies eat the seeds, while mule deer, elk and moose browse its foliage.

Mexican white pine (opposite) is a variety of the limber and intergrades with it in southwestern New Mexico, southeastern Arizona and northern Mexico at elevations from 6,500' to 10,000'.

178

Mexican White Pine

Arizona, border or Southwestern white pine; border limber pine, ayacahuite pine, pino enano [dwarfish pine]

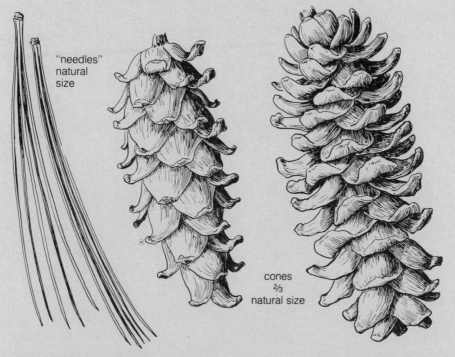

"needles" natural size

cones ⅔ natural size

Pinus flexilis var. *reflexa*

Pine family *(Pinaceae)*

Range: se AZ, sw NM, w. TX; s. to Mex. Mountain canyons, 6,500' - 10,000'.

This pine is distinguished from limber pine (opposite), as well as from all other pines, by the strongly reflexed tips of the cone scales. In all other respects it closely resembles its ancestor, the limber pine. Where this pine and limber pine overlap in their distribution, they integrade freely and it is hard to tell one from the other.

Mexican white pine is one of the least known of the white pines in the Southwest because of its scattered distribution in relatively inaccessible places. In overall aspect it looks like limber pine in exposed places, but grows tall and straight in more favorable situations.

Like all white pines, its pale, blue green needles are in bundles of 5. The needles are from 3 to 4 inches long, whereas the needles of limber pine are from 1½ to 3 inches long.

It was first discovered in Chihuahua, Mexico in 1846, but not until 1874 was it found in the United States in the Santa Rita Mountains of Arizona.

Rocky Mountain Bristlecone Pine

foxtail pine

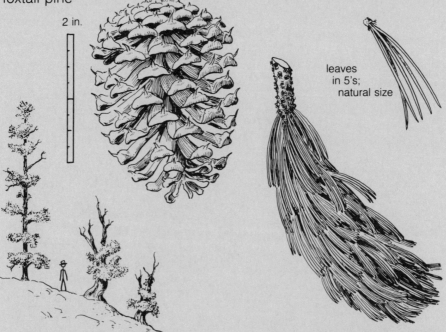

2 in.

leaves
in 5's;
natural size

Pinus aristata   Pine family _(Pinaceae)_

Range: Of limited, but widely scattered distribution, AZ, NM, CO. In thin, rocky soils, 7,500' - 11,500'.

One of our 5-needled pines, sharing with limber pine the highest wind-swept ridges, and often confused with it. It can be distinguished from the limber pine by its smaller cones with incurved prickles or bristles on the tips of the cone scales (p. 105), which give the tree its name. The name "foxtail" is derived from the fact that the twigs are densely clothed with needles and resemble a fox's bushy tail.

Because it grows in high, windy places, old trees are often twisted into very picturesque shapes (p. 108). Weather-beaten dead trunks are even more gnarled, and weathered to a silvery sheen (p. 108).

Bristlecone pines have a life span, measured not in hundreds of years, but in thousands! Annual rings have been counted to 4,600, which means that some were already over 2,600 years old at the time of the birth of Christ. They were even over 1,100 years old when the Egyptians were building the pyramids, making them the oldest living things on earth!

The bristlecone pine of CA, NV and UT is now considered to be a separate species, Great Basin bristlecone pine: _Pinus longaeva_.

Lodgepole Pine

"doghair" pine, "tamarack" pine

natural size

Pinus contorta var. *latifolia*   Pine family *(Pinaceae)*

Range: NM, CO, UT; w. to CA; n. to AK; s. to Mex. Moist or dry disturbed soils, 5,000' (n.) and 7,500' - 11,500' (s.).

The lodgepole pine grows tall and slim, and its long, slender trunks were used by the Indians as tepee, or lodge poles, hence its common name. These poles were also used as travois shafts lashed to either side of a horse, one end dragging on the ground. This device was used for hauling their tepees and household goods.

The trees grow in dense, even-aged groves "thick as hairs on a dog's back." They are so crowded together that it is almost impossible to push through them. The trunk diameter is commonly no more than a foot, with "doghair" stands averaging more like 5 to 6 inches. In such groves, the trees seldom exceed 75 feet in height and bear branches only near their tops.

The bark is usually scaly and dark gray in dense stands, but orange brown in more open groves. The mature female cones (p. 105) produce the seeds but remain closed for years (unless squirrels cut them off while they are still green). The seeds retain their vitality until the heat of a forest fire pops open their long-closed scales, spilling the seeds to the ground — one of nature's ways of reseeding fire-swept areas.

The male "flowers" (p. 105) produce pollen to fertilize the female cones.

Lodgepole pine's spindly trunks serve well as fenceposts and fence rails, corral posts and for telephone poles.

Myrtle Blueberry

mountain blueberry, huckleberry, whortleberry, myrtle whortleberry, mirtillo [little myrtle]

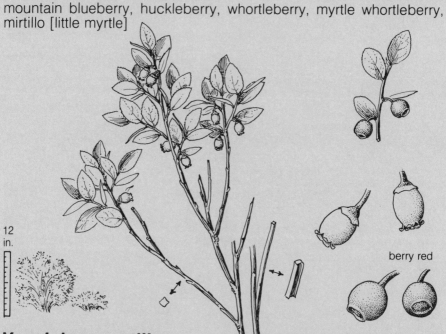

12 in.

berry red

Vaccinium myrtillus

Heather family *(Ericaceae)*

Range: AZ, NM, CO, UT; w. to CA; n. to Can.; also Eu. & n. Asia. Dense forest floors, 8,000' - 12,000'.

Myrtle blueberry is a low, sprawling, deciduous shrub with myrtlelike leaves, usually about 6 to 18 inches tall, growing mostly in the higher mountains. The branchlets are green and have 3 to 4 wings. The bushes often form quite extensive solid carpets under the forest trees. Thin and translucent leaves cover the shrub.

Its small, waxy, urn-shaped flowers are pink and white and bloom in early summer, ripening to bluish black berries by late summer. They are juicy and sweet, and are not only delicious when eaten fresh from the bushes, but have long been used to make very good pies, tarts, jellies, puddings, syrups and wines. They are often mixed with apples, peaches or other fruits for delightfully different taste treats. One cannot fail to enjoy muffins and pancakes made with blueberries. The leaves have been used to make a tea. It has been in cultivation since 1789.

It is interesting to note how some plant names are derived: early Americans were not botanists, so they transferred foreign names to the unknown plants that they encountered, as: wort, whort, whortle, whortleberry; hurt, hurtle, hurtleberry; thence our huckleberry.

Wolf Currant

black currant

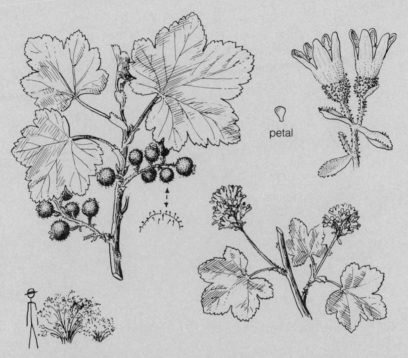

petal

Ribes wolfii

Saxifrage family *(Saxifragaceae)*

Range: AZ, NM, CO, UT; n. to WY. Moist woods & gravelly, open slopes, 6,000' - 11,500'.

This is the more common currant of the higher parts of the Uplands. Its flowers are small, yellowish white bells, sometimes tinged with pink, and grow in small clusters. The fruits, about ½ inch in size, are blackish with a bloom. They are sticky and bristly when young, but fortunately the bristles fall off as they ripen. The fruits are rather tasteless, tart, and sometimes bitter, but make excellent jellies and pies.

Songbirds, chipmunks, ground squirrels and other animals also eat them. Elk have been known to browse the foliage. Indians used dried currants as one of the ingredients of pemmican.

All currants are hosts for white pine blister rust, and for this reason, efforts have been made to eradicate them in white pine country. Cultivation of currants, therefore, has been discouraged.

The dried currant of commerce is a sharp-flavored raisin.

Waxflower

cliffbush, cliff jamesia, mountain mockorange, wild hydrangea

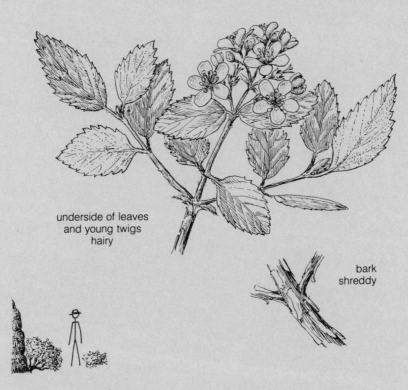

underside of leaves
and young twigs
hairy

bark
shreddy

Jamesia americana   Saxifrage family *(Saxifragaceae)*

Range: AZ, NM, CO, UT; w. to CA; n. to WY. Moist cliffs & cliff bases and along streams, 5,500' - 10,000'.

    This is one of our most attractive native shrubs growing to about 3 or 4 feet high. It has waxy white, slightly fragrant, mockorange-like flowers, but with 5 petals instead of 4 as in the mockorange. Its serrated leaves are dark green above and downy white below. The bark is reddish brown and somewhat shreddy, and its young shoots are fuzzy white, shading to brown.

    Adding to the autumnal coloring of the Uplands, its leaves turn beautiful shades of red. It becomes a fine ornamental shrub when grown in city gardens because of its attractive, fragrant flowers and fall foliage.

    It is a "pioneer" plant, usually starting its growth in cliff crevices. Together with mockorange, it is a member of the saxifrage family, but placed by some in the hydrangea family.

Bebb Willow

beaked willow, sauce, sauz

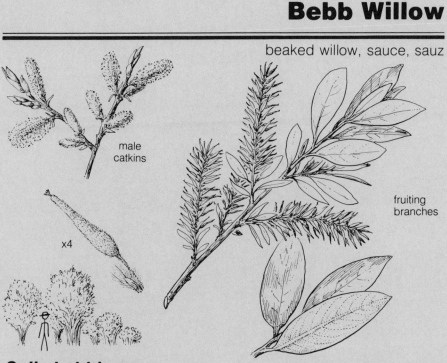

male catkins

x4

fruiting branches

Salix bebbiana

Willow family *(Salicaceae)*

Range: AZ, NM, CO, UT; w. to CA; n. to AK; e. to Atl. Coast. Along streams & in wet ground, 8,000' - 11,000'.

The most common willow of this belt grows along streams, lakeshores and in wet ground, from the foothills to nearly treeline. It is also one of the most widespread, occurring from Alaska, across Canada to Labrador; from California, across our area and northeast to Nebraska and Iowa; and east to Maryland and New England.

It is naturally a tall shrub, but may reach tree size, but seldom exceeds 10 to 20 feet. In thickets in marshy areas, more often than not, it is kept browsed down to 2 or 3 feet by deer, moose and elk. Beavers not only eat it, but also use it for building materials. Cottontail rabbits nibble the young shoots, and grouse as well as deer eat the flower buds.

Its grayish green bark is often tinged with red and has shallow furrows and flat ridges. Other features which help to identify this species is its dull green leaves, silvery white and net-veined below; leaves widest at their middles; and leaf margins *not* toothed.

As with most willows and poplars, its bark is bitter because of the presence of salicin. This bitter principle is extracted from the barks of both willow and poplar and used medicinally to relieve fever, pain and rheumatism. The Kiowa Indians chewed the bark of willows to relieve toothache.

185

Treeline "Trees"

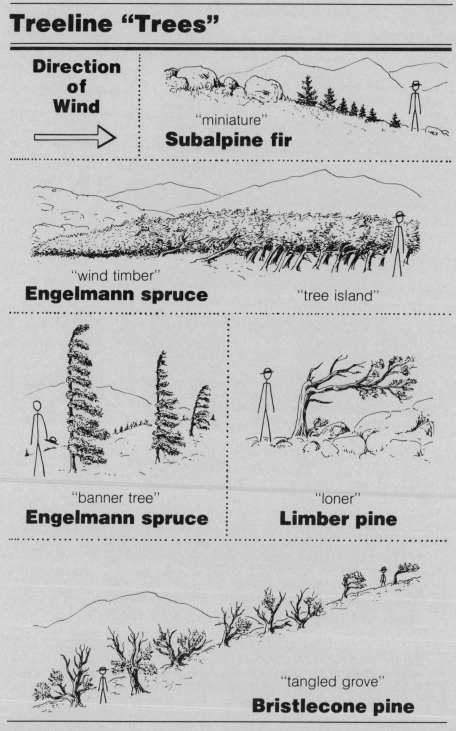

Direction of Wind →

"miniature"
Subalpine fir

"wind timber"
Engelmann spruce

"tree island"

"banner tree"
Engelmann spruce

"loner"
Limber pine

"tangled grove"
Bristlecone pine

Treeline[1]

(Approx. 11,500')[2]

As the elevations, roughly between 10,500 and 11,500 feet are reached, trees become smaller and smaller until they are no more. As these limits are attained, the trees become more and more buffeted by the nearly incessant high-velocity, drying winds and subjected to very low temperatures.

In this most inhospitable habitat, below-freezing temperatures are frequent, even in midsummer, and snowstorms may occur at any time. This makes for a very short growing season of approximately 90 days, hardly long enough for seeds to be produced. The winters, therefore, are long and cold. The soil, too, is cold and much of the moisture falls as snow and is unavailable to plants except in the spring as it melts. The climate, consequently, is very similar to that near the Arctic Circle or in the Alps and the belt is called the Alpine or Arctic-Alpine Life Zone. Treeline is its lower boundary.

Snowdrifts remain throughout the summer, as they are so solidly packed that they melt very slowly; however, except for the more protected places, most of the snow is melted by August. About a month later snowstorms arrive again to start the accumulations anew.

Subalpine fir, the bristlecone and limber pines, and the Engelmann spruce are the only trees that can survive at these windy, frigid heights, sometimes assuming grotesque forms.

Subalpine fir *(Abies lasiocarpa)* is the only one of these trees that retains its shape — becoming a reduced miniature of itself, even though no more than a foot or two high.

Engelmann spruce *(Picea engelmannii),* contrastingly, forms masses of scrubby thickets just a few feet high called "tree islands" or "wind timber" (p. 108). These stunted mats result because, in winter, twigs above the snow are killed, while those below the snow are able to survive. Sometimes so tightly woven is this matting that one individual cannot be distinguished from another. Just below these tangled masses, the Engelmann spruce may assume another entirely different form: it becomes a "banner" tree (p. 108), so-called because its branches stream out from the leeward side of the trunk much like a banner blowing in the breeze. This is largely due to desiccation of the buds on the windward side of the tree.

Limber pine *(Pinus flexilis),* in contrast, is a "loner" — a gnarled old individual standing isolated and bent at right angles — preferring to live in majestic solitude in exposed, windswept places.

Bristlecone pine *(Pinus aristata),* on the other hand, grows in gnarled, open groves (p. 108), or sometimes singly (p. 108), with twisted torsos fashioned by the frequent gales. Their trunks are often scoured free of bark on the windward side by the granular snow borne by the icy winds of winter, or by the sand-laden winds at other seasons.

Shrubs such as myrtle blueberry, redberried elder and trumpet gooseberry may be found at, and beyond, treeline.

[1] Treeline, rather than timberline, is used here as a more accurate term, since usable "timber" ceases to grow hundreds of feet below the last gnarled and stunted tree.

[2] Treeline is very irregular and occurs higher on the warm, south-facing slopes and lower on the cold, north-facing slopes.

Identification Chart for Evergreens

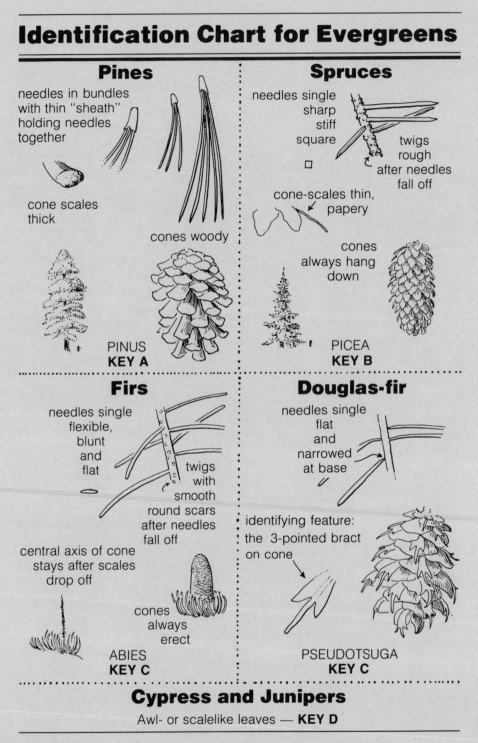

Pines

needles in bundles with thin "sheath" holding needles together

cone scales thick

cones woody

PINUS
KEY A

Spruces

needles single
sharp
stiff
square

twigs rough after needles fall off

cone-scales thin, papery

cones always hang down

PICEA
KEY B

Firs

needles single
flexible,
blunt
and
flat

twigs with smooth round scars after needles fall off

central axis of cone stays after scales drop off

cones always erect

ABIES
KEY C

Douglas-fir

needles single
flat
and
narrowed
at base

identifying feature: the 3-pointed bract on cone

PSEUDOTSUGA
KEY C

Cypress and Junipers

Awl- or scalelike leaves — **KEY D**

188

Keys to the Evergreens

Key A — Pines

(Needles in bundles with thin "sheath" holding needles together; cone scales thick and woody)
Four choices:
1. Needle single with sheath . . . . Singleleaf pinyon, p. 18
2. Needles in twos (two choices):
   a. Trees, tall, growing in mountains . . . . Lodgepole pine, p. 105, 181
   b. Trees small, on desert edges . . . . Pinyon pine, p. 14, 105
3. Needles in threes (four choices):
   a. Needles under 2 inches long (Mexican border) . . . . Mexican pinyon, p. 19
   b. Needles 2 to 4 inches long (Mexican border) . . . . Chihuahua pine, p. 20
   c. Needles 5 to 8 inches long (widespread) . . . . Ponderosa pine, p. 98, 110
   d. Needles 10 to 15 inches long (Mexican border) . . . . Apache pine, p. 113
4. Needles in fives (two choices):
   a. Cone scales bristle tipped,
      needles ¾ to 1½ inches long . . . . Bristlecone pine, p. 105, 108, 180
   b. Cone scales not bristle tipped (two choices):
      (1): Needles 3 to 4 inches long (Mexican border) . . . . Arizona pine, p. 110
      (2): Needles 1 to 3 inches long (two choices):
         (a): Cone scales normal (widespread) . . . . Limber pine, p. 107, 178
         (b): Cone scales strongly turned back
              (Mexican border) . . . . Mexican white pine, p. 179

Key B — Spruces

(Needles single, sharp, stiff and square; cone scales thin and papery; cones always hang down)
Two choices:
1. Bark reddish, platy; cones about 2½ inches long . . . . Englemann spruce,
                                                                        p. 104, 108, 174
2. Bark gray, scaly; cones over 2½ inches long . . . . Blue spruce, p. 177

Key C — Firs

(Needles single, soft and flat)
Two choices:
1. Cones pendant; 3-toothed bracts projecting from between the
   cone scales . . . . Douglas-fir, p. 105, 158
2. Cones erect; no bracts (two choices):
   a. Needles 2 or more inches long . . . . White fir, p. 160
   b. Needles about an inch long (two choices):
      (1): Bark hard . . . . Subalpine fir, p. 105, 106, 175
      (2): Bark soft, corky . . . . Corkbark fir, p. 176

Key D — Cypress & Junipers

(Needles awl- or scalelike)

Two choices:

1. Fruit woody; scales separating at maturity . . . . Arizona cypress, p. 115
2. Fruit fleshy; scales remaining fused at maturity (two choices):
   a. Low spreading shrub . . . . Common juniper, p. 96, 161
   b. Small trees (two choices):
      (1). Bark broken into squares . . . . Alligator juniper, p. 16
      (2). Bark stringy or shreddy (two choices):
         (a). Berries marble size . . . . Utah juniper, p. 15, 96
         (b). Berries pea size (two choices):
            (i). Berry juicy, mostly 1-seeded . . . . One-seed juniper, p. 17
            (ii). Berry dry, usually
                 2- or 3-seeded. . . . . Rocky Mountain Juniper, p. 96, 114

Pronunciation and Translation of Scientific (Latin) Names

(Including Greek, French, Carib, Japanese, etc. derivatives which have all been latinized)

It is next to impossible to communicate plant identification by using common names. One species of plant may have different common names in different parts of the country; conversely different species of plants may have the same common name in other parts. To put order in this confusion caused by the use of common names throughout the world — in hundreds of languages and dialects — scientists long ago started using Latin names for all plants and animals. This is known as a system of binomial nomenclature in which each species of plant or animal receives a name consisting of two Latin words (or latinized words from other languages), the first of which identifies the genus to which it belongs and the second, the specific or species name. Occasionally a variety is designated: the system then becomes trinomial.

A scientist from Spain, for instance, could exchange Latin names with a colleague from Japan, although each would use a slightly different accent; however, they would understand each other most of the time.

Carl von Linné (latinized to Carolus Linnaeus), a Swede, known as the founder of modern plant classification was deeply involved in the Latin system of nomenclature. When he travelled in 1735 and 1736 to Germany, Holland, England and France he used Latin as an international language, and was understood everywhere he went.

Presently, Latin is truly a "foreign" language, and the layman can only hazard a guess as to correct pronunciation. But there is no avoiding Latin names if one wants to be positive in one's identification of a plant or animal. It is hoped that users of this book would like to know something of the pronunciation and origin of the scientific names, as it piqued my curiosity, even though some of the names were almost unpronounceable and some nearly untranslatable.

There seems to be no set of comprehensive rules intelligible to the layman for the pronunciation of botanical names. Even some of the best authorities disagree on some points. A partial list of references is appended.

How Latin names are pronounced really matters little provided that they are understood by all concerned. You are most likely to be understood if you stick to the classical Latin pronunciation, but who nowadays is versed in classical Latin. For those interested I have here used a modified American (English) version, since most people using this book will tend to pronounce Latin by analogy with the words of their own language.

It is the Latin generally used by gardeners and lay botanists who are not "purists," and I'm in this class. For instance, in "pure" Latin every vowel is pronounced, and -*oides,* from the Greek meaning "like or resembling" should be pronounced -oh-EYE-deez, but is more often than not pronounced as if "oi" were a diphthong, i.e., -OY-deez. This is my preference and is used throughout the list in this manner. [The -oh-EYE-deez pronunciation is also shown for the die-hards.]

If the reader is this far along in this discourse, then perhaps a few general rules are in order:

1. Syllables (Words must be broken into syllables before they can be accented):
a. In dividing a Latin word into syllables, a single consonant is joined to the vowel which follows it, as *Senecio:* se-ne´-ci-o (seh-NEE-sih-oh). [N.B.: the phonetic

(foh-NET-ik) pronunciation is given with the accented syllable in CAPITAL LETTERS.]

      b. If two or more consonants occur together, division is before the last consonant: *stansburiana:* stans-bu-ri-a´-na (stanz-buh-rih-AY-nuh).

      c. Exception: if b, c, d, g, k, p or t is followed by l or r, both go with the following vowel, as *glabra:* gla´-bra (GLAY-bruh).

      d. ch, ph and th are considered single letters.

2. Accents:

      a. Words of two syllables are always accented on the first syllable, as *Acer:* A´-cer (AY-ser).

      b. Words of three or more syllables are accented on the next-to-last syllable if that is long, as *Arbutus:* Ar-bu´-tus (are-BEW-tuss), otherwise on the third-from-last: *Abies:* A´-bi-es (AY-bih-eez).

3. Vowels (All vowels are pronounced and are either short or long):

Vowel	Short as in:	Written as:	Long as in:	Written as:
a	mat	a	mate	ay
e	met	eh	me	ee
i	bit	ih	bite	eye
o	not	o	note	oh
u	cut	uh	cute	yew
y	symbol	ih	by	eye

(Note: an "a" ending a word, and occasionally beginning a word, is written as "uh," as *Amorpha* (uh-MOR-fuh); all other final vowels are long, as *-aceae* [-AY-see-ee]).

4. Diphthongs (Two vowels written together and pronounced as one):

Diphthong	As in:	Written as:
ae	Caesar	ee
ai*	rail	ay
au	auk	aw
ei	height	eye
eu	feud	yew
ia*	Asia	uh
oe	bee	ee
oi*	oil	oy
ou*	soup	oo
ui	ruin	ew

*Not accepted as diphthongs by purists.

5. Consonants:

      c is hard before a, o, oi or u as in cat and written as k

      c is soft before ae, e, i, oe or y as in cent and written as s

      cc followed by i or y as in occident is written as k-s

      ch is hard as in chorus and written as k

      g is hard before a, o, oi or u as in go and written as g

      g is soft before ae, e, i, oe or y as in gem and written as j

      ph is pronounced as in phase and written as f

      s is pronounced as in English *except* when it comes between two vowels *(Compositae, Rosa),* when it is final and preceded by n or r *(repens)* or ending after "ie" as in *Abies,* when it is pronounced as in rose, and written as z

      x is hard as in extra and written as ks

      x as an initial letter as in Xerox is pronounced as z

      In paired consonants, as *Ptelea,* the first letter is silent: TEE-lee-uh.

Epilogue

In order to stick as nearly as possible to the original pronunciations of the names honoring persons and to "modernize" some pronunciations, a few rules have been slightly bent, as follows:

1. Accents have been moved so that the names can be pronounced as nearly as possible like the original, but with Latin endings: *knowltonii:* NOHL-tun-eye [nohl-TUN-ih-eye].

2. "ia" is usually pronounced as a diphthong: *Purshia:* PURSH-uh [PURR-shih-uh].

3. "ii" is usually pronounced as a single "i": *gambelii:* GAM-bull-eye [gam-BEH-lih-eye].

4. "oi" is pronounced as a diphthong, as: *betuloides:* bet-yew-LOY-deez [beh-tyew-loh-EYE-deez].

Bibliography for Scientific (Latin) Names

BAILEY, LIBERTY HYDE
    n.d. *How Plants Get Their Names.* Dover Publications, N.Y., NY.
BAILEY, RALPH, Editor
    1948. *The Home Garden Self-Pronouncing Dictionary of Plant Names.* The American Garden Guild, N.Y., NY.
BORRER, DONALD J.
    1963. *Dictionary of Word Roots and Combining Forms.* 3rd Printing. N-P Publications, Palo Alto, CA.
FLORISTS' PUBLISHING CO.
    1974. *Dictionary of Plant Names.* 12th Printing. Chicago, IL.
JAEGER, EDMUND C.
    1955. *A Source-book of Biological Names and Terms.* 3rd edition. Charles C Thomas, Publisher, Springfield, IL.

    1960. *The Biologist's Handbook of Pronunciations.* Charles C Thomas, Publisher, Springfield, IL.
OSTERMAN, Georg F. von
    1952. *Manual of Foreign Languages.* 4th edition, revised & enlarged. Central Book Co., Inc., N.Y., NY.
PLOWDEN, C. CHICHELEY
    1970. *A Manual of Plant Names.* 2nd edition, revised. Philosophical Library, N.Y., NY.
RADFORD, ALBERT E., DICKISON, WILLIAM C., MASSEY, JIMMY R. & BELL, C. RITCHIE
    1974. *Vascular Plant Systematics.* Harper & Row, Publishers, N.Y., Evanston, San Francisco, London.
STEARN, WILLIAM T.
    1966. *Botanical Latin. History, Grammar, Syntax, Terminology and Vocabulary.* Hafner Publishing Co., N.Y., NY.
SMITH, A. W.
    1963. *A Gardener's Book of Plant Names: A Handbook of the Meanings and Origins of Plant Names.* Harper & Row, Publishers, N.Y., NY.
WEBSTER'S BIOGRAPHICAL DICTIONARY. 1st edition.
    1969. G. & C. Merriam Co., Publishers, Springfield, MA.

Pronunciation and Translation of Scientific (Latin) Names

(All words are of Latin origin unless otherwise noted)

Abies: AY-beez [AY-bih-eez; A-bih-eez]. The silver fir tree.

-aceae: -AY-see-ee. Ending added to the name of the type genus to form the family name; as *Rosaceae* from *Rosa.*

Acer: AY-ser [A-ser]. The maple tree. The word is perhaps related to "sharp", "pointed" or "cutting" in reference to the hardness and firmness of the wood which · the Romans used for spears.

Aceraceae: ay-suh-RAY-see-ee [a-suh-RAY-see-ee]. The maple family.

acerosa: a-seh-ROH-suh. Needle-shaped; needlelike.

acuminata: a-kew-mih-NAY-tuh. Tapering to a point; acuminate.

Alnus: AL-nuss. The alder tree. "Alder" comes from Old English *alor, aler* with phonetic "d" added.

Amelanchier: a-meh-LAN-kih-err. A French name for a related plant, the medlar-tree whose fruit was eaten when decayed.

americana: uh-meh-rih-KAY-nuh. Of or from America.

Amorpha: uh-MOR-fuh. Of indefinite form; shapeless; referring to the absence of 4 of the 5 petals. [Greek].

amygdaloides: uh-mig-duh-LOY-deez [a-mig-duh-loh-EYE-deez]. Almond- or peach-like, referring to the leaves.

Anacardiaceae: a-nuh-kar-dih-AY-see-ee. Greek: the cashew (sumac) family, from the heartlike shape of the top of the fruit stem of the cashew.

angustifolia(-um): an-gus-tih-FOH-lih-uh(-um). Narrow- or slender-leaved.

anomala: uh-NAH-muh-luh. Unusual; abnormal; irregular; inconsistent; deviating from the common type; anomalous.

Arbutus: are-BEW-tuss. The European strawberry-tree (arbute).

Arctostaphylos: ark-toh-STAFF-ih-los. Greek for bear and grape cluster, as bears feed on the clustered berries.

argentea: are-JEN-teh-uh. Silvery; silvered.

aristata: a-riss-TAY-tuh. Provided with awns; bristly; bearded; aristate; in reference to the long slender prickles on the cone scales of the bristlecone pine.

arizonica: a-rih-ZOH-nih-kuh. Of or from Arizona.

Artemisia: are-teh-MEE-sih-uh [are-teh-MIH-sih-uh]. In honor of the sister and wife of Mausolus, king of Caria. Artemisia was known as a botanist and medical researcher, having discovered and named several herbs. She built a magnificent tomb (4th cent. B.C.) for her husband. It was known as one of the seven wonders of the ancient world and brought the word "mausoleum" into our language.

Atriplex: A-trih-pleks. The Greek name for orache, a species of this genus which can be used as spinach, but which is generally regarded as a weed.

aureum: AW-reh-um. Golden [yellow].

baccata: bak-KAY-tuh. Berrylike.

Baccharis: BAK-kuh-riss. Ancient Greek name for an unknown plant with a fragrant root yielding oil, supposed to be good against enchantments and transferred to this genus by Linnaeus.

bebbiana: BEBB-ih-AY-nuh Michael S. Bebb (1833-95), noted student of willows.

Berberidaceae: ber-beh-rih-DAY-see-ee. The barberry family (See below).

Berberis: BER-beh-riss. Latinized from an Arabic name for the fruit of the barberry.

Betula: BEH-tyew-luh [BEH-tuh-luh]. The birch tree.

Betulaceae: beh-tyew-LAY-see-ee [beh-tuh-LAY-see-ee]. The birch family.

betulaefolia: beh-tyew-lee-FOH-lih-uh [beh-tuh-lee-FOH-lih-uh]. Birchleaved.

betuloides: beh-tyew-LOY-deez [beh-tyew-loh-EYE-deez]. Birchlike.

Bouvardia: boo-VAR-dih-uh. In honor of French physician to Louis XIII, Charles Bouvard (1572-1658), at one time superintendent of the Royal Botanic Gardens in Paris.

brandegei: BRAN-deh-gee-eye [bran-DEE-jee-eye]. In honor of Townsend S. Brandegee (1843-1925), prominent western self-trained botanist and student of Mexican flora.

Brickellia: brik-KELL-lih-uh. In honor of Dr. John Brickell (1749-1809), Irish-American botanist and naturalist of Savannah, Georgia who published, in 1787, *A Natural History of North Carolina.*

Cactaceae: kak-TAY-see-ee. Applied by the ancient Greeks to some prickly plant, *kaktos,* possibly the Spanish artichoke; adopted by Linnaeus for the cactus family.

californica: kah-lih-FOR-nih-kuh. Of or from California.

canescens: kuh-NESS-senz. Becoming grayish; hoary; gray-hairy; canescent.

Caprifoliaceae: kap-rih-foh-lih-AY-see-ee. Goat [-hoofed?] -leaved.

Ceanothus: see-uh-NOH-thuss. An obscure name, originally applied to a spiny plant, perhaps a thistle, but not this plant.

Celastraceae: see-lass-TRAY-see-ee. An ancient Greek name for some evergreen shrub, perhaps holly or privet. Species name adopted for the bittersweet family. Also called burningbush or stafftree family.

Celtis: SELL-tiss. Pliny's name for an African species of *Lotus,* transferred to this genus perhaps on account of the sweet berries.

cembroides: sem-BROY-deez [sem-broh-EYE-deez]. Like the Swiss stone pine *(Pinus cembra).*

Cephalanthus: seh-fuh-LAN-thuss. Greek for head-flower, as the flowers are in spherical heads.

Cercis: SUR-siss. Ancient Greek name for a kind of poplar; also, perhaps the Judas-tree of Europe and Asia.

Cercocarpus: sur-koh-KAR-pus. Greek: shuttle-fruit, referring to its long-tailed fruit.

Chamaebatiaria: kah-mee-bah-tih-AY-rih-uh. Greek: like *Chamaebatia,* the ground or creeping bramble.

Chenopodiaceae: keh-noh-poh-dih-AY-see-ee [key-noh-poh-dih-AY-see-ee]. Greek for goose-foot, in reference to the shape of the leaves of members of this family.

chihuahuana: chih-wah-wah-AY-nuh. Of or from Chihuahua, Mexico, where it was first discovered. It was first described by Dr. George Engelmann (See *engelmannii*) in 1848.

Chrysothamnus: krih-soh-THAM-nuss. Greek for golden-bush.

Clematis: KLEH-muh-tiss [KLEE-ma-tiss]. Ancient Greek for a climbing plant with long, lithe twigs or shoots, probably the periwinkle. Transferred by Linnaeus to the *Clematis* [occasionally klee-MA-tiss].

coerulea: see-REW-leh-uh. Deep blue; sky blue; azure; cerulean; in reference to the fruits. Originally the deep blue of the Mediterranean sky at midday.

Coleogyne: koh-lee-AH-jih-nee. Greek: sheathed-ovary, referring to the tubular sheath which encloses the ovary.

communis: kom-MEW-niss. Widespread; general; common.

Compositae: kom-PAH-zih-tee. "To bring several together in a orderly manner;" composite; in reference to the florets which are arranged in dense heads that resemble single flowers. The composite or sunflower family.

concolor: KON-kuh-luhr. Of the same color; uniform in color; of one color throughout; in reference to the needles of the white fir.

confertifolia: kon-fer-tih-FOH-lih-uh. Crowded-leaves; leaves pressed close together; densely leaved.

contorta: kon-TOR-tuh. Twisted; bent; contorted.

Cornaceae: kor-NAY-see-ee. Dogwood family. (See next).

Cornus: KOR-nuss. The cornelian cherry *(Cornus mas)* of Europe, from the word for horny, in reference to the hardness of the wood in some species which was used for spears, shafts and javelins.

Cowania: kow-WAY-nih-uh. In honor of James Cowan (d. 1823), early British merchant and amateur botanist who introduced many plants from Mexico and Peru into England.

Crataegus: kra-TEE-gus. Greek for a kind of thorny flowering shrub, possibly a holly, and perhaps related to the word for "strength," in reference to the hardness and toughness of the wood.

Cupressus: kew-PRESS-suss. Latin and Greek for the Italian cypress.

cuspidata: kuss-pih-DAY-tuh. Sharp; stiff-pointed; cuspidate; in reference to the leaf apex.

Dalea: DAY-leh-uh. In honor of Dr. Samuel Dale (1659-1739), English physician, botanist and author.

demissa: duh-MISS-uh. Lowly; humble; drooping.

deppeana: DEPP-peh-AY-nuh [depp-peh-AY-nuh]. In honor of Ferdinand Deppe (d. 1861), German botanist who had given this species a name previously used for another species.

douglasii: DUGLUSS-eye [duh-GLAH-sih-eye]. In honor of David B. Douglas (1798-1834), Scottish botanist and collector for the Royal Horticultural Society of London who spent several years collecting in Oregon. A squirrel was also named in his honor. (See also *Garrya*).

drummondii: DRUM-mund-eye [drum-MUN-dih-eye]. In honor of Thomas Drummond (1780-1835), Scottish explorer and botanist in North America who first discovered it.

dumosa(-us): dew-MOH-suh(-us). Bushy; shrubby.

edulis: EH-dyew-liss. Fit to eat; edible.

Elaeagnaceae: eh-lee-ag-NAY-see-ee. Elaeagnus family. (See next).

Elaeagnus: eh-lee-AG-nuss. Greek for olive tree and chaste tree *(Vitex agnus-castus)*. *Agnus* also translates "lamb," "pure," or "innocent."

elata: ee-LAY-tuh. Tall or elevated.

emarginata: ee-mar-jih-NAY-tuh. Having a shallow notch at tip (emarginate), in reference to the petals and sepals.

emoryi: EMORY-eye [eh-MORE-ee-eye]. In honor of Major (later Lt. Col.) William H. Emory (1811-1887), who collected many new specimens during his Military Reconnaissance of 1848. He later became director of the U. S.-Mexican Boundary Survey (1857-59).

engelmannii: ENGULL-mun-eye [en-gull-MUN-nih-eye]. In honor of Dr. George Engelmann (1809-1884), German-born botanist and researcher of St. Louis. He had an active medical practice, but also carried on botanical and meteorological work. Authority on dodder, cacti and grapes. He was one of the first physicians to use quinine as a specific against malaria.

Ephedra: eh-FEH-druh [eh-FEE-druh]. Greek for mare's-tail which it resembles.

Ephedraceae: eh-feh-DRAY-see-ee [eh-fee-DRAY-see-ee]. Joint-fir family. (See above).

Ericaceae: eh-rih-KAY-see-ee. Latin and Greek for the heather family.

Eriodictyon: eh-rih-oh-DICK-tee-on [ee-ree-oh-DICK-tee-on]. Greek: woolly network, referring to the woolly, netted undersurfaces of the leaves.

Eriogonum: eh-rih-AW-guh-num [ee-ree-AW-guh-num]. Greek for woolly and knees, referring to the hairy nodes in some species.

erythropoda: eh-rih-THRAH-puh-duh. Greek: reddish-footed, perhaps for the reddish leaf petioles.

Eurotia: yew-ROH-shuh [yew-ROH-tee-uh]. Greek, in reference to the gray white, downy or moldy appearance.

exigua: eks-IH-joo-uh [eks-IH-gew-uh]. Very small, short, insignificant in reference to the small-size leaves.

Fagaceae: fay-GAY-see-ee. The beech family, from the word "to eat," in reference to the edible beechnuts.

Fallugia: fal-LEW-jih-uh. In honor of Virgilio Falugi, an Italian abbot of Vallombrosa and a botanical writer.

Fendlera: FEND-lurr-uh. In honor of August Fendler (1813-1883), German-born naturalist and explorer who settled in the U.S. and was one of the first botanists to collect in Texas, New Mexico and Venezuela.

Fendlerella: FEND-lurr-ell-uh [fen-dluh-RELL-uh]. Little fendler plant. (See above).

fendleri: FEND-lurr-eye [FEN-dluh-rye]. Of Fendler. (See *Fendlera*).

filifolia: fih-lih-FOH-lih-uh. Threadlike (filiform) leaves.

flavescens: flay-VESS-senz. Becoming yellow; pale yellow; yellowish; in reference to the foliage.

flexilis: FLEKS-ih-liss. Pliable; supple; limber; flexible; in reference to the flexible branches of limber pine.

Forestiera: faw-ress-tih-EH-ruh [faw-ress-tih-EE-ruh]. In honor of Charles Le Forestier, 18th century French physician and naturalist of Saint-Quentin.

formosa: for-MOH-suh. Finely formed; handsome; beautiful; shapely; in reference to flowers.

Frankenia: FRANK-ee-nih-uh [fran-KEE-nih-uh]. Named by Linnaeus in honor of Johann Francke (latinized to Frankenius) (1590-1661), a Swedish professor of medicine at Uppsala who was the first to describe the plants of Sweden.

Frankeniaceae: FRANK-ee-nih-AY-see-ee [fran-kee-nih-AY-see-ee]. Frankenia family. (See above).

Fraxinus: FRAKS-ih-nuss. The ash tree. From Greek, to hedge or enclose, as the ash was formerly used for hedges.

fremontii: FREE-mont-eye [free-MON-tih-eye]. In honor of John Charles Frémont (1813-1890), soldier, explorer and naturalist of western U. S. and one of the first two United States senators from California. He was the first botanist to collect in the Sierra Nevada on two expeditions to California, 1843-4 and 1845-7. From 1878 to 1882 he was governor of Arizona Territory.

fruticosa: frew-tih-KOH-suh. Shrubby; shrublike; bushy.

gambelii: GAM-bull-eye [gam-BEH-lih-eye]. In honor of Dr. William Gambel (1819-1849), Philadelphia ornithologist and botanist who collected in the West in the 1840s. His name is also perpetuated in the name of the Gambel quail, as well as in three other birds.

Garrya: GAIR-ree-uh. In honor of Nicholas Garry, secretary of the Hudson's Bay Company, friend of David Douglas (See *douglasii*), botanical explorer of the Pacific Northwest, 1825-32, who named this genus after his friend who assisted him greatly in his collecting.

glaberrima: glah-BEHR-rih-muh. Very smooth; very glabrous.

glabra(-um): GLAY-bruh(-um). Smooth, without hairs; glabrous.

Glossopetalon: gloss-soh-PEH-tuh-lon. Greek: tonguelike petals.

glutinosa: glew-tih-NOH-suh. Sticky; gluey; glutinous.

grandidentatum: gran-dih-den-TAY-tum. Large-toothed, referring to the leaf margins.

grandiflora: gran-dih-FLOH-ruh. Large-flowered.

Grayia: GRAY-uh [GRAY-ih-uh]. In honor of Asa Gray (1810-1888), professor of botany at the University of Michigan, and later professor of natural history at Harvard — a distinguished American botanist and early authority on western plants. A member of the Hall of Fame.

greggii: GREGG-eye [GREGG-gih-eye]. In honor of Dr. Josiah Gregg (1806-1850), adventurer, trader and botanical explorer in northern Mexico and adjacent U. S. Author of *Commerce of the Prairies,* a narrative about the Old Santa Fé Trail.

grisea: GRIH-sih-uh. Pearl gray.

Gutierrezia: goo-tih-ehr-REE-zih-uh. In honor of Pedro Gutiérrez, correspondent of the Botanic Garden of Madrid, Spain.

Haplopappus: ha-ploh-PAPP-pus. [Sometimes spelled *Aplopappus*]. Greek for single and down (pappus), in reference to the simple hairs on the seeds.

Holodiscus: hah-loh-DISS-kuss. Greek: entire or undivided disk, as some related genera have lobed disks.

Hydrophyllaceae: hye-droh-fill-LAY-see-ee. Greek: waterleaf family. The leaves of waterleaf supposedly catch rain and hold it in specialized cavities.

hypoleucoides: hye-poh-lew-COY-deez [hye-poh-lew-coh-EYE-deez]. Greek: whitish beneath, in reference to the leaves.

idaeus: eye-DEE-us. Of Mount Ida, highest peak in Crete, now called Mt. Psiloriti. The infant Jupiter was raised here.

imbricata: im-brih-KAY-tuh. Overlapping in regular order like tiles or shingles.

incana: in-KAY-nuh. Quite gray; grayish white; hoary.

inebrians: ih-NEE-brih-anz. Intoxicating.

inerme: ih-NURR-muh. Unarmed; without thorns, spines or prickles.

integerrimus: in-teh-GEHR-rih-muss. Very whole; absolutely entire; very perfect; unbroken; referring to the leaves.

involucrata: in-voh-lew-KRAY-tuh. Provided with a group or whorl of bracts (involucre) which envelop the base of the inflorescence.

Jamesia: JAYMZ-ih-uh. [juh-MEE-zee-uh]. In honor of Dr. Edwin James (1797-1861), physician-botanist-historian to Long's Expedition to the Rocky Mountains in 1819-1820. With two others, he made the first ascent of Pike's Peak. The genus is sometimes called by his first name, *Edwinia.*

jamesii: JAYMZ-eye [juh-MEE-zee-eye]. (See above).

Juglandaceae: joo-glan-DAY-see-ee. The walnut family. (See *Juglans*).

Juglans: JOO-glanz. Jupiter's acorn *[Jovis glans].*

Juniperus: joo-NIH-peh-russ. The juniper tree. [Originally *iuniperus*].

knowltonii: NOHL-tun-eye [nohl-TUN-ih-eye]. In honor of Frank H. Knowlton, distinguished paleobotanist with the U. S. Geological Survey who discovered this species of hophornbeam in the Grand Canyon.

Labiatae: lay-bih-AY-tee. Having two unequal parts shaped like lips; labiate. The mint family.

lanata: luh-NAY-tuh. Woolly; woollike; flannellike; lanate.

laricifolius: luh-rih-sih-FOH-lih-us. Larch-leaved.

lasiocarpa: la-sih-oh-KAR-puh. Greek: shaggy-, hairy-, woolly fruited.

latifolia: la-tih-FOH-lih-uh. Wide- or broad-leaved.

ledifolius: lee-dih-FOH-lih-us. Leaves like *Ledum,* the Labrador tea.

Leguminosae: leh-gew-mih-NOH-see. Pea or legume family, containing plants bearing pealike pods used as food. The original Latin meant "to gather or pick."

leiophylla: lye-oh-FILL-luh. Greek: smooth-leaved.

leptanthum: lep-TAN-thum. Greek: slender-flowered.

ligusticifolia: lih-guss-tih-sih-FOH-lih-uh. Leaves like the *Ligusticum,* the lovage of our gardens.

Liliaceae: lih-lih-AY-see-ee. The classical Latin name (from Greek) for the lily family.

longiflorus: lon-jih-FLOH-russ. Long-flowered.

longilobus: lon-JIH-loh-buss. Long-lobed, in reference to the leaves.

Lonicera: lah-NIH-seh-ruh. In honor of Adam Lonitzer (latinized to Lonicerus) (1528-1586), German physician and botanist (herbalist) who held the position of "pensioned naturalist" in Frankfurt-am-Main, Germany for 32 years.

198

Lycium: LIH-sih-um. An ancient Greek name for a prickly shrub found growing in Lycia, an ancient region in Asia Minor (now applied to Turkey in Asia). Its juice and roots were used medicinally.

macropetala: ma-kroh-PEH-tuh-luh. Large-petalled.

major: MAY-johr. Refers to greater or larger size.

melanocarpa: meh-la-noh-KAR-puh. Greek: very dark or black-fruited.

Menodora: meh-noh-DOH-ruh. Greek: gift and force, in reference to the force or strength that it supposedly gave animals who ate it.

menziesii: MEN-zeez-eye [men-ZEE-sih-eye]. In honor of Archibald Menzies (1754-1842), Scottish surgeon and naturalist who accompanied Vancouver on his expedition to the Pacific Northwest (1790-95). He collected, among other plants, the original specimen of Douglas-fir from Vancouver Island.

microphylla(-us): mye-kroh-FILL-luh(-us). Little- or small-leaved.

millefolium: mill-leh-FOH-lih-um. Thousand-leaved [i.e., many-leaved].

monogynus: mah-NAH-jih-nuss. Greek: one-style.

monophylla: mah-noh-FILL-luh. Greek: one-leaved [i.e., -needled].

monosperma: mah-noh-SPER-muh. Greek: one-seeded.

montanus: mon-TAY-nuss. Growing on mountains; montane.

montigenum: mon-TIH-jeh-num. Mountain-born, in reference to its mountainous habitat.

Moraceae: moh-RAY-see-ee. The mulberry family.

Morus: MOH-russ. The mulberry tree.

myrsinites: murr-sih-NYE-teez. Greek: myrtlelike.

myrtillus: murr-TILL-luss. Little-myrtle, in reference to its small myrtlelike foliage; or perhaps in honor of Myrtillus, son of Mercury and a charioteer.

nauseosus: naw-seh-OH-sus. L. & Gr.: ship-sickness; producing sickness; nauseating.

navajoa: na-vuh-HOH-uh. From the Navajo country; specifically, the Navajo Indian Reservation.

negundo: neh-GUN-doh. A Dravidian word for the Old World box elder *(Vitex negundo)*. Dravidian is a language of India, Ceylon and West Pakistan with no established relationship to any other.

neomexicana(-us): nee-oh-meks-ih-KAY-nuh(-us). Of or from New Mexico.

occidentalis: ok-sih-den-TAY-liss. Of or from the West or western hemisphere.

Oleaceae: oh-lee-AY-see-ee. The olive [oil] family.

Opuntia: oh-PUN-shuh [oh-PUN-tih-uh]. A cactuslike plant "of Opus," an ancient city in Greece, but now applied to our prickly pear cacti.

oreophilus: oh-reh-oh-FIH-luss. L. & Gr: mountain-loving.

Ostrya: OSS-trih-uh. L. & Gr. for some tree with very bony (hard) wood, perhaps the hornbeam.

Oxytenia: oks-ih-TEE-nih-uh. Sharp-pointed, referring to the leaves.

Pachystima: puh-KISS-tih-muh. Greek: with a thick stigma.

pallidum: PAL-lid-um. Rather-pale; pallid; gray green; yellow green.

paradoxa: pa-ruh-DOK-suh. L. & Gr: contrary to belief or expectation; strange; contrary to type; unexpected; in reference to the paradoxical resemblance of the flowers of Apache-plume to a single, white rose.

Parryella: PARRY-ella [pa-rih-ELL-luh]. Diminutive parry, in honor of Dr. Charles C. Parry (1823-1890), English-born botanist and physician who collected for the U. S.-Mexican Boundary Survey, 1854-58.

Parthenocissus: parr-theh-noh-SISS-suss. L. & Gr: virgin-ivy, of no known application.

parviflorus: parr-vih-FLOH-russ. Small-flowered.

patula: PA-tyew-luh. Spreading; broad; wide.

pentandra: pen-TAN-druh. Greek: five-stamened.

Philadelphus: fih-luh-DELL-fuss. In honor of Egyptian King Ptolemy II (Philadelphus) (309?-246? B.C.), of no obvious application, but possibly because he did so much to beautify the cities of his kingdom. He was founder of the great Alexandrian library.

Physocarpus: fye-soh-KAR-puss. Greek: bladder or bellows fruit, in reference to its inflated (bladderlike) pods.

Picea: PYE-see-uh. The pitch pine or spruce. [L. & Gr: made of pitch].

Pinaceae: pye-NAY-see-ee. The pine family.

pinetorum: pye-neh-TOH-rum. Of pine forests or groves.

Pinus: PYE-ness. The pine tree.

Platanaceae: plah-tuh-NAY-see-ee. The sycamore or planetree family.

Platanus: PLAH-tuh-nuss. The planetree. Related to Greek for broad or flat, in reference to the leaves.

pluriflorus: plew-rih-FLOH-russ. Several-flowered; many-flowered.

Poliomintha: poh-lih-oh-MIN-thuh. Grayish white (hoary) mint.

Polygonaceae: poh-lih-goh-NAY-see-ee. Many-knees, from the numerous swollen stem joints. The buckwheat family.

ponderosa: pon-deh-ROH-suh. Of great weight; heavy; massive; stately; ponderous. Name suggested in 1826 by David Douglas (for whom the Douglas-fir was named — see *douglasii*), because of its massive bulk.

Populus: POP-pew-luss. The poplar [cottonwood] tree. Possibly from "people," from the number and continual motion of its leaves.

Potentilla: poh-ten-TILL-luh. Somewhat powerful, in reference to its supposed medicinal properties.

Prunus: PREW-nuss. The plum tree.

pseudoalpina: soo-doh-al-PYE-nuh. Greek: resembling, but not equaling and alpine; false-alpine.

Pseudotsuga: soo-doh-TSOO-guh. A curious combination of Greek and Japanese for false and hemlock.

Ptelea: TEE-lee-uh. Greek for the [wing-fruited] elm tree, because this genus has fruits like the elm.

pungens: PUN-jenz. Sharp-pointed; prickly; pungent.

Purshia: PURSH-uh [PURR-shih-uh]. In honor of Friedrick Pursh (originally Frederich T. Pursch) (1774-1820), botanist. He was born in Germany, but spent many years in North America and wrote the first complete flora (1814) of America north of Mexico based on the plants collected by the Lewis and Clark expedition. Curator of botanical gardens at Baltimore and New York.

Quercus: KWUR-kuss. The oak tree, which was sacred to Jupiter.

racemosa: ra-seh-MOH-suh. Bearing flowers in an elongated cluster (raceme).

radicans: RA-dih-kanz. Having stems which take root.

ramosissima: ra-moh-SISS-sih-muh. Very-much branched.

Ranunculaceae: ra-nun-kew-LAY-see-ee. Little frog [tadpole], suggesting the marshy habitat of the buttercup family.

reflexa: reh-FLEKS-uh. Bent sharply backward; reflexed at more than 90°.

repens: REE-penz. Creeping; prostrate and rooting.

reticulata: reh-tih-kew-LAY-tuh. Netted; net-veined; reticulate; as veins in leaves.

Rhamnaceae: ram-NAY-see-ee. The buckthorn family. (See next).

Rhamnus: RAM-nuss. An ancient Greek name for the buckthorn, akin to the Greek word for rod.

Rhus: RUSS. An ancient Greek and Latin name for the European smoke tree *(Rhus cotinus)*; sumac(h).

Ribes: RYE-beez. An ancient name of uncertain origin, but probably Arabic for a plant with a sour sap. Related to Danish *ribs* and German *Riebs*, names for the currant.

rivularis: rih-view-LAY-riss. Pertaining to a brooklet or rivulet, referring to a preference for moist banks of small streams.

Robinia: roh-BIH-nih-uh. In honor of Jean Robin (1550-1629), herbalist to Henry IV of Navarre in French Pyrenees, and his son Vespasien (1579-1662), who first introduced the locust tree into Europe.

Rosa: ROH-zuh. The rose bush.

Rosaceae: roh-ZAY-see-ee. The rose family.

rotundifolia(-us): roh-tun-dih-FOH-lih-uh(-us). Round-leaved.

Rubiaceae: rew-bih-AY-see-ee. The madder family, from the Latin for red; madder; from the use of the roots for making a moderately strong red dye.

Rubus: REW-buss. The bramble bushes, but related to Latin for red.

rupicola: rew-PIH-koh-luh. Rock-, cliff-, crag-dwelling.

Rutaceae: rew-TAY-see-ee. The rue family, from both Latin and Greek.

Salicaceae: say-lih-KAY-see-ee. The willow family.

Salix: SAY-liks. The willow tree.

Sambucus: sam-BEW-kuss. An ancient Greek name for the elder because parts of a medieval stringed instrument [sambuke] were sometimes made from its wood.

Sapindaceae: sa-pin-DAY-see-ee. The soapberry family. (See next).

Sapindus: sa-PIN-duss. Latin for soap and India, referring to the use of its berries as soap in the West Indies.

Saponaria: sa-poh-NAY-rih-uh. Soapy; soap-producing.

Sarcobatus: sar-koh-BAY-tuss. Greek: fleshy and thorny, with reference to its fleshy leaves and thorny stems.

sargentii: SAR-jent-eye [sar-JEN-tih-eye]. In honor of Dr. Charles S. Sargent (1841-1927), American dendrologist and first director of the Arnold Arboretum at Harvard.

sarothrae: suh-ROH-three. Greek: broom, esp. one made of twigs.

Saxifragaceae: saks-ih-fra-GAY-see-ee. The saxifrage family, from Latin, stone and break, as many species root in clefts of rocks. Saxifrage is considered by some to be a remedy for gall stones [Stone-breaker?].

scabra: SKAY-bruh. Rough; gritty; scurfy; scabrous; in reference to leaf surfaces.

schottii: SHOTT-eye [SHOTT-tih-eye]. In honor of Arthur Schott, American naturalist connected with various early government surveys.

scopulorum: skaw-pew-LOH-rum. Of rocky places, cliffs or crags.

scouleriana: SKOOLER-ih-AY-nuh [skoo-leh-rih-AY-nuh]. In honor of Dr. John Schouler (1804-1871), Scottish naturalist who collected in northwest United States, 1825-27.

Senecio: seh-NEE-sih-oh. Old-man, referring to the white hairlike pappus of many species.

sergiloides: ser-jih-LOY-deez [ser-jih-loh-EYE-deez]. Like *Sergilus,* the old name for *Baccharis.*

Shepherdia: sheh-PURD-ih-uh. In honor of English botanist John Shepherd (1764-1836), former curator of the Liverpool Botanic Gardens.

Solanaceae: soh-luh-NAY-see-ee. The nightshade (potato) family, perhaps related to Latin: solace or quieting, as some members of the family have narcotic properties, as belladonna.

Sorbus: SOR-buss. The service-tree of Europe, or the mountain-ash.

spartioides: spahr-tih-OY-deez [spahr-tih-oh-EYE-deez]. Broomlike.

spinescens: spye-NESS-senz. Slightly spiny; spinescent; thorny.

Spiraea: spye-REE-uh. Greek: garland or wreath, for which some species may have been used.

stansburiana: STANZ-burr-ih-AY-nuh [stanz-buh-rih-AY-nuh]. In honor of Capt. (later Major) Howard Stansbury (1806-1863), leader of the U. S. government's exploration to the Great Salt Lake area. He collected the first specimen of *Cowania* on Stansbury Island in the lake in 1852.

stolonifera: stoh-luh-NIH-feh-ruh. Producing runners that take root (stolons).

strigosus: strih-GOH-suss [strye-GOH-suss]. Having meager or few hairs; strigose.

Symphoricarpos: sim-foh-rih-KAR-pus. Greek: fruit-borne-together, from the clustered berries.

Tamaricaceae: ta-muh-rih-KAY-see-ee. The tamarisk family. (See below).

Tamarix: TA-muh-riks. The tamarisk, possibly in reference to the Tamaris River in Spain, along which it is reported to grow.

tenuifolia: teh-nyew-ih-FOH-lih-uh. Thin-leaved.

Tetradymia: teh-truh-DIH-mih-uh [teh-truh-DYE-mih-uh]. Greek: four-together, in reference to the four-flowered heads.

thesioides: theh-sih-OY-deez [theh-sih-oh-EYE-deez]. Greek: like *Thesium,* the bastard toadflax with which Theseus crowned Ariadne, his wife.

torreyana: TORREY-ay-nuh [torr-ree-AY-nuh]. In honor of Dr. (M.D.) John Torrey (1796-1873), emeritus professor of botany and chemistry at College of Physicians and Surgeons, New York, authority on many groups of plants. He identified and named many plants for John C. Frémont. (See *fremontii*).

tremuloides: treh-mew-LOY-deez [treh-mew-loh-EYE-deez]. Resembling the European quaking aspen *(Populus tremula)* whose leaves tremble or quake.

tridentata: trye-den-TAY-tuh. Three-toothed, in reference to the leaves.

trifoliata: trye-foh-lih-AY-tuh. Three-leaved.

trilobata: trye-loh-BAY-tuh. Three-lobed, referring to the leaves.

turbinella: tur-bih-NELL-luh. Little-top(-shaped), referring to the acorns of the oak.

Ulmaceae: ull-MAY-see-ee. The elm family, from *Ulmus,* the elm.

umbellatum: um-bell-LAY-tum. Umbrellalike (clusters of flowers).

undulata: un-dyew-LAY-tuh. Wavy(-edged), in reference to the leaves.

utahensis: yew-taw-EN-siss. Of or from Utah.

uva-ursi: OO-vuh-URR-see [YEW-vuh-URR-sye]. Grape plus bear; bearberry.

Vaccinium: vak-SIH-nih-um. The whortleberry, but the name is of disputed origin. Thought, by some, to have come from Latin "of or from cows," referring to their fondness for the plant; in fact, an Old World species is called "cowberry."

velutina: veh-LYEW-tih-nuh. Velvety, in reference to the leaves.

vermiculatus: verr-mih-kew-LAY-tuss. Worm-shaped, referring to the spiral seed embryos.

virginiana: verr-jih-nih-AY-nuh. Of or from Old Virginia which was much more extensive than the present-day Virginias.

viridis: VIH-rih-diss. Green, in reference to the stems.

viscidiflorus: viss-sih-dih-FLOH-russ. Sticky-flowered.

vitacea: vye-TAY-see-uh. Vine- or grapelike.

Vitaceae: vye-TAY-see-ee. The grape family.

Vitis: VYE-tiss. The (grape) vine.

wislizenii: wiss-lih-ZEEN-eye [wiss-lih-ZEE-nih-eye]. In honor of Frederick A. Wislizenus [VISS-lih-SAY-noos] (1810-1899), German-born physician and naturalist of St. Louis who collected in the 1840s and 1850s in the southwest and Mexico.

wolfii: WOLF-eye [WOL-fih-eye]. In honor of John Wolf (1820-1897), German-born field assistant with Wheeler's Expedition. He collected nearly all of the plants for the expedition in 1873.

woodsii: WOODZ-eye [WOOD-zih-eye]. In honor of Joseph Woods (1776-1864), English botanist and student of the roses.

wrightii: RIGHT-eye [RIGHT-ih-eye]. In honor of Charles Wright (1811-1885), botanist in the Southwest in the 1840s and 1850s while a member of the U. S.-Mexican Boundary Survey.

Yucca: YUKK-kuh. The Carib name *(yuca)* for the root of the cassava plant from which tapioca is made, perhaps because the yucca of the Southwest also has similar large roots.

List of Abbreviations

Appendix III

AK	Alaska	N. Am.	North America
Alta.	Alberta	NB	Nebraska
Atl.	Atlantic	NC	North Carolina
AR	Arkansas	ND	North Dakota
AZ	Arizona	ne	northeast
c.	central	Nfld.	Newfoundland
CA	California	NJ	New Jersey
Can.	Canada	NM	New Mexico
CO	Colorado	NV	Nevada
d.	died	NY	New York
Daks	ND & SD	nw	northwest
ed.	edition	OH	Ohio
elev.	elevation	OK	Oklahoma
Eng.	England	OR	Oregon
esp.	especially	PA	Pennsylvania
Eu.	Europe	Que.	Quebec
FL	Florida	rev.	revised
GA	Georgia	s.	south
Gnld.	Greenland	S. Am.	South America
Gr.	Greek	Sask.	Saskatchewan
Gt. Brit.	Great Britain	sc	southcentral
IA	Iowa	SD	South Dakota
ID	Idaho	Sp.	Spanish
IL	Illinois	sw	southwest
KS	Kansas	TX	Texas
L.	Latin	U. S.	United States
LA	Louisiana	UT	Utah
Lab.	Labrador	VA	Virginia
Mex.	Mexico	var.	variety
MI	Michigan	w.	west
MO	Missouri	WA	Washington
MT	Montana	W. Indies	West Indies
n.	north	WY	Wyoming

Selected References

ARNBERGER, LESLIE P. and JANISH, JEANNE R.
 1968. *Flowers of the Southwest Mountains.* 4th Ed. Southwest Parks and Monuments Assoc., Globe, AZ.

BENSON, LYMAN and DARROW, ROBERT A.
 1954. *The Trees and Shrubs of the Southwestern Deserts.* Univ. of Arizona Press, Tucson and Univ. of New Mexico Press, Albuquerque, NM.

BERRY, JAMES BERTHOLD
 1966. *Western Forest Trees* (Reissued). Dover Pubs., N.Y., NY.

CORRELL, DONOVAN S. and JOHNSON, MARSHALL C.
 1970. *Manual of the Vascular Plants of Texas.* Texas Research Foundation, Renner, TX.

DODGE, NATT N. and JANISH, JEANNE R.
 1973. *Flowers of the Southwest Deserts.* 8th Ed., Rev. Southwest Parks and Monuments Assoc., Globe, AZ.

ELMORE, FRANCIS H.
 1944. *Ethnobotany of the Navajo.* Univ. of New Mexico Press and School of American Research, Albuquerque, NM.

HARRINGTON, HAROLD D.
 1964. *Manual of the Plants of Colorado.* 2nd Ed. Sage Books, The Swallow Press, Inc., Chicago, IL.

HARRINGTON, HAROLD D. and MATSUMURA, Y.
 1971. *Edible Native Plants of the Rocky Mountains.* The Univ. of New Mexico Press, Albuquerque, NM.

JOHNSON, CARL M.
 1970. *Common Native Trees of Utah.* Utah State Univ., Logan. Special Report No. 22.

KEARNEY, THOMAS H. and PEEBLES, ROBERT H.
 1960. *Arizona Flora.* 2nd Ed. Univ. of California Press, Berkeley, CA.

LAMB, SAMUEL H.
 1971. *Woody Plants of New Mexico.* New Mexico Dept. of Game and Fish Bulletin No. 14.

LITTLE, ELBERT L., Jr.
 1953. *Check List of Native and Naturalized Trees of the United States (Including Alaska).* Agriculture Handbook No. 14, U. S. Govt. Printing Office, Washington, DC.

 1968. *Southwestern Trees.* Agriculture Handbook No. 9 (Reprint). U. S. Govt. Printing Office, Washington, DC.

MARTIN, ALEXANDER C., ZIM, HERBERT S. and NELSON, ARNOLD L.
 1961. *American Wildlife and Plants.* Dover Publications, N.Y., NY.

PATRAW, PAULINE M. and JANISH, JEANNE R.
 1970. *Flowers of the Southwest Mesas.* 5th Ed. Southwest Parks and Monuments Assoc., Globe, AZ.

PEATTIE, DONALD CULROSS
 1953. *A Natural History of Western Trees.* Bonanza Books, N.Y., NY.

PRESTON, RICHARD J., Jr.
 n.d. *Rocky Mountain Trees.* (Reprint of original edition published in 1940). Dover Publications, N.Y., NY.

SARGENT, CHARLES SPRAGUE
 1947. *The Silva of North America.* (Reprinted 1947). Peter Smith, N.Y., NY.

1965. *Manual of the Trees of North America*. (Reprint). Dover Pubs., N.Y., NY.

TIDESTROM, IVAR

    1925. *Flora of Utah and Nevada*. Contributions from the U. S. National Herbarium, Vol. 25, U. S. Govt. Printing Office, Washington, DC.

VINES, ROBERT A.

    1960. *Trees, Shrubs and Woody Vines of the Southwest*. Univ. of Texas Press, Austin.

WEBER, WILLIAM A.

    1972. *Rocky Mountain Flora*. 4th Ed., Rev. Colorado Associated University Press, Boulder.

WOOTON, E. O. and STANDLEY, P.C.

    1915. *Flora of New Mexico*. Contributions from the U. S. National Herbarium, Vol. 19, Smithsonian Institution, Washington, DC.

YANOVZKY, ELIAS

    1936. *Food Plants of the North American Indians*. U. S. Department of Agriculture Misc. Pub. No. 237. U. S. Govt. Printing Office, Washington, DC.

Index

NOTE: **Accepted common names** and **page references** to the color illustrations are in **heavy type;** *Latin names* are in *italicized heavy type; Latin family names* and *synonyms* are in *italics;* and other common names are in regular type.

206

213

Credits

Edited by . . . . .Earl Jackson, Globe, Arizona
Technical editor . .Dr. Charles T. Mason, Jr., Tucson, Arizona
Designed by . . . . . . .Christina Watkins, Denver, Colorado
Printed by . . . . .Lorraine Press, Salt Lake City, Utah
Typography by . . . .Denver Type & Design, Inc., Denver, Colorado
Type style . . . . .Helvetica, a clean modern Swiss letterform designed
for easy reading.